I0467621

Financial Terms Dictionary

Banking Terminology Explained

Published July 01, 2017

Revision 1.1

Financial Terms Dictionary

Copyright And Trademark Notices

Limits of Liability and Disclaimer of Warranties

The materials in this book are provided "as is" and without warranties of any kind either express or implied. The Author disclaims all warranties, express or implied, including, but not limited to, implied warranties of merchantability and fitness for a particular purpose.

The Author does not warrant that defects will be corrected, or that that the site or the server that makes this eBook available are free of viruses or other harmful components. The Author does not warrant or make any representations regarding the use or the results of the use of the materials in this book in terms of their correctness, accuracy, reliability, or otherwise. Applicable law may not allow the exclusion of implied warranties, so the above exclusion may not apply to you.

Under no circumstances, including, but not limited to, negligence, shall the Author be liable for any special or consequential damages that result from the use of, or the inability to use this eBook, even if the Author or his authorised representative has been advised of the possibility of such damages.

Applicable law may not allow the limitation or exclusion of liability or incidental or consequential damages, so the above limitation or exclusion may not apply to you. In no event shall the Author's total liability to you for all damages, losses, and causes of action (whether in contract, tort, including but not limited to, negligence or otherwise) exceed the amount paid by you, if any, for this eBook.

Facts and information are believed to be accurate at the time they were placed in this book. All data provided in this book is to be used for information purposes only. The information contained within is not intended to provide specific legal, financial or tax advice, or any other advice whatsoever, for any individual or company and should not be relied upon in that regard. The services described are only offered in jurisdictions where they may be legally offered. Information provided is not all-inclusive, and is limited to information that is made available and such information should not be relied upon as all-inclusive or accurate.

You are advised to do your own due diligence when it comes to making business decisions and should use caution and seek the advice of qualified professionals. You should check with your accountant, lawyer, or professional advisor, before acting on this or any information. You may not consider any examples, documents, or other content in this eBook or otherwise provided by the Author to be the equivalent of professional advice.

The Author assumes no responsibility for any losses or damages resulting from your use of any link, information, or opportunity contained in this book or within any other information disclosed by the author in any form whatsoever.

About the Author

Thomas Herold is a successful entrepreneur and personal development coach. After a career with one of the largest electronic companies in the world, he realised that a regular job would never fully satisfy his need for connection on a deep level. The only way to live his full potential was to start building his own business and find new ways to be in service to others.

For over 25 years he has helped many people - including himself - build their dream businesses. Toward that goal, he focuses on education, simplified and enhanced by modern technology. He is the author of 15 books with over 200,000 copies distributed worldwide.

Other than his passion for creating businesses, Thomas has spent over 20 years in the self-development field. Placing emphasis on the exploration of consciousness and building practical applications that allow people to express their purpose and passion in life, Thomas's work in this area has provided ample and happy proof that this approach works.

He believes that every person has at least one gift and that, when this gift is developed and nourished, it will serve as a fountainhead of personal happiness and help contribute to a better, more sustainable world.

For the past twelve years Thomas has studied the monetary system and has experienced some profound insights on how money and wealth are related. He has recently committed to sharing this financial knowledge in a new venture - the Financial Terms Dictionary, a hub of financial term descriptions designed to help people get started on their own money makeover and get a financial education in the process.

Thomas's ultimate vision for the Financial Terms Dictionary is to empower people to adopt a wealthy mindset and to create abundance for themselves and others. His ability to explain complex information in simple terms makes him an outstanding teacher and coach.

For more information please visit: Financial Terms Dictionary

Financial Dictionary Series

There are 12 books in this financial dictionaries series available. Click the links below to see an overview and available formats. There is also a premium edition available, which covers over 900 financial terms!

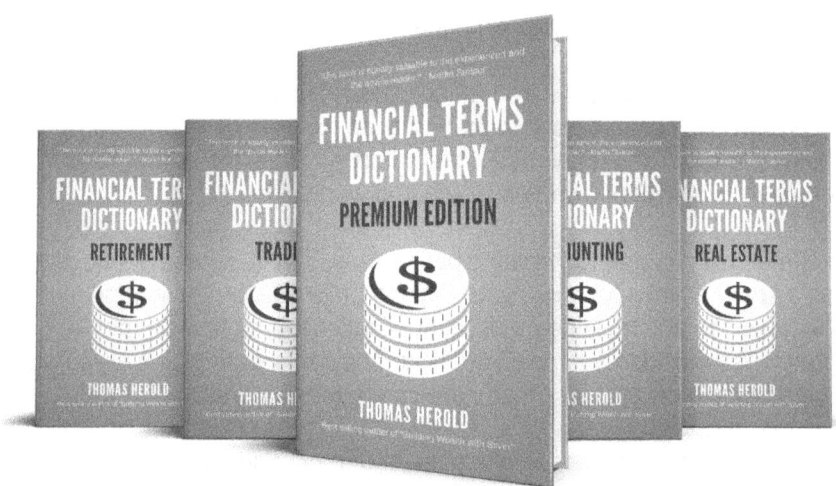

Standard Editions
Financial Terms Dictionary - Accounting Edition
Financial Terms Dictionary - Banking Edition
Financial Terms Dictionary - Corporate Finance Edition
Financial Terms Dictionary - Economics Edition
Financial Terms Dictionary - Investment Edition
Financial Terms Dictionary - Laws & Regulations Edition
Financial Terms Dictionary - Real Estate Edition
Financial Terms Dictionary - Retirement Edition
Financial Terms Dictionary - Trading Edition
Financial Terms Dictionary - Acronyms Edition

Basic & Premium Editions
Financial Terms Dictionary - Basic Edition
Financial Terms Dictionary - Premium Edition

Table Of Contents

American Institute of Banking (AIB)

The American Institute of Banking (AIB) is a venerable educational and training institution for the United States based banking industry which was established by the American Bankers Association (ABA) back in 1907.

This AIB offers continuing training and a full range of banking career education for parties who are interested in the banking field or who are already participants within it. Over 150,000 existing bankers take part in their extensive range of continuing educational programs every year. As such, the AIB is the definitive and universally recognized continuing education curriculum for those within the fields of financial services.

American Institute of Banking programs were created to boost, refresh, and improve the job skills and knowledge base of those working in or seeking to work within the financial services industry. Completing some of these degreed programs can provide a path to AIB certificates and even diplomas which are universally recognized within the banking realm. They can also help with obtaining required professional licenses.

These programs encompass more than the traditional open enrollment programs provided throughout all of the various states. The AIB of today also offers convenient digital format purchase of its services and products, training provided in-house and Internet-based provision of online classes and coursework, tests, and study teams classes. These are only a few of the many options for its in-depth and extensive industry-wide programs.

The American Institute of Banking falls under the umbrella of the founder American Bankers Association. This means that all AIB programs and courses are provided through the local area branches of the ABA and its providers. Among its many classes and programs are core courses in such fields as business fundamentals; general banking; consumer, commercial, and mortgage lending; retail banking; asset management; compliance issues; and marketing.

In-bank branch training utilizes instructions and resources to offer specifically tailored delivery of the various ABA training regimens within a banker's own branch. It might also be offered off site in the immediate area, depending on demand.

In recent years, the American Institute of Banking has moved aggressively into the digital age with its instructional offerings. Thanks to this decision, they now offer Internet-based online versions of their best selling, traditional instructor-driven AIB courses. They provide extensive information, schedules, and enrollment forms for this mode of education on their website.

The American Institute of Banking offers certificate programs which it tailored to help participants boost their knowledge of and performance in banking utilizing course curriculum which has been bank tested for a specific bank focus. These courses run the gamut across a variety of skill sets and content and each complement the other. Certificate-driven courses are shorter in length and typically run from one to three weeks in total duration.

The American Institute of Banking also provides full-scale banking diplomas. These are awarded for successfully completing both required and elective option courses. Courses which provide at least two hours of credit award traditional grade levels of A, B, C, or D. In order for courses to count towards one of the AIB diplomas, students must receive a C or higher overall average. One course can be utilized towards one or multiple certificates or diplomas.

The ABA has recently decided to roll up the separately branded AIB into its own proprietary programs. All American Institute of Banking courses are now provided as a division of ABA Training. These courses, whether offered in person or online, generally meet the requirements mandated by the ICB Institute of Certified Bankers for continuing education credits and appropriate exams. The ABA online training was designed specifically to be cost affordable and flexible. This is why they aim to constantly update the information and learning experienced which is now able to be accessed at any time, from any place.

Bailout

Bailouts prove to be the action of handing money or other capital to a company, individual, or nation that will likely go down without help. This is done in an effort to keep the entity from financial insolvency, bankruptcy, or total failure. Sometimes bankruptcies are pursued to permit an organization to fail without panic, so that fear and systemic failure does not become endemic, taking down other similar entities along the way.

Various different groups might qualify for urgent bailouts. Countries like Greece have been prime examples in the year 2010. Companies such as major banks and insurance outfits have been deemed too big to fail in the several years preceding 2010, during the height of the financial crisis and resulting Great Recession. Other industries have qualified as well, including car manufacturers, airlines, and vital transportation industries.

A good example of companies that receive preferential bailout treatment lies in the transportation industry. The Untied States government believes that transportation proves to be the underlying core of the nation's economic versatility, necessary to support the country's geopolitical power.

Because of this, the Federal Government works to safeguard the largest companies involved in transportation from failing with low interest rate loans and subsidies, which are a form of bailout. Oil companies, airlines, railroads, and trucking companies could all be considered to be a critical part of this industry. Such firms are considered to be too big and important to fail because their services prove to be nationally and constantly necessary to support the country's economy and thereby its eventual security.

Bailouts that are done in an emergency fashion typically prove to be full of controversy. In 2008 in the United States, intense and angry debates erupted regarding the failing banking and car manufacturing businesses. The camp standing against such bailouts looked at them as a means of passing the expensive bill for the failures over to the taxpayers.

Leaders of this group savagely denounced any monetary bailouts of the big three car makers and large banks, which they said all needed to be broken up as punishment for mismanagement. They criticized a new moral hazard that was being created by guaranteeing safety nets to other businesses. They similarly did not like the big central bureaucracy that arises from government agencies selecting the size and disposition of the bailouts. Finally, government bailouts of these groups were attacked as a form of corporate welfare that continues the cycle of more corporate irresponsibility.

The other camp argued that these bailouts were necessary evils, since the state of the American economy did not prove to be solid enough to suffer the failure of either the major banks or the car makers. With the car makers, fully three million jobs stood on the line. The banking industry had the argument of systemic failure of the financial system backing it up. No one on the side of the bailouts pretended to like having to engage in them, but they were said to be necessary nonetheless. In the end, such bailouts were issued to both major industries totaling in the trillions of dollars.

Cash Savings Account

A cash savings account is a place that you can park your cash and gain interest on it. Effective short term savings accounts are ones that permit you to meet your needs in four important areas. The access to the funds is critical.

Cash savings accounts should allow you to withdraw funds from the account whenever you need. This should be accomplished through convenient methods like ATM cards or online means. Funds in all types of cash savings accounts are insured by the FDIC, or Federal Deposit Insurance Corporation, to $100,000 for all people and $250,000 for retiree accounts.

Interest is another area of concern for cash savings accounts. This pertains to the rate that the bank or institution will give you for holding your money. Larger amounts generally attract superior rates.

Penalties should not have to be endured for withdrawing cash from cash savings accounts either. Certificates of Deposits and other instruments feature such penalties, but cash savings accounts should not. These terms of withdrawal should be clearly specified in any cash savings account.

Finally, service is an issue to be considered with cash savings accounts. You might wish to have customer service in a bank branch included. Otherwise, do it yourself online accounts can be established.

There are several types of cash savings accounts from which you can choose. One is a checking account that includes interest. This might be called a money market account. Such money market accounts include check writing privileges and check based access to funds. These can be held at banks or brokerage houses, which are gaining in popularity at banks' expense. Some privileges besides check writing include higher money market rates of interest and ATM card and machine access to funds. Downsides to these types of accounts include sometimes high minimum balances and possible fees.

Standard savings accounts are another option with cash savings accounts. These were once called passbook accounts. The interest rates provided by these accounts are lower than inflation, which proves to be their major downside. Their major advantage lies in the extremely low account minimums and fees charged to have them.

High yield bank accounts are a third type of cash savings accounts. Providing versatility of adding or withdrawing funds without penalties, they also offer the liquidity of not tying up your money for long periods of time. Nowadays, there are high yield bank accounts that provide interest rates that prove to be comparable to Certificates of Deposits, without showcasing these investments' restrictions on taking out money. The highest rates available on high yield bank accounts come from banks that are online only versions of the traditional lending institutions.

They accomplish this by not offering branches and in person customer service benefits. This means that unless such an online high yield account includes an ATM card, the only way to withdraw the funds is through electronic transfers to other brokerage, savings, or checking accounts, which can result in delays of as much as two to five full days. Without such an ATM card, it can be inconvenient to access cash stored in these accounts in a hurry or emergency situation. High yield accounts sometimes offer shorter term teaser interest rates, so individuals should investigate the product's prior six month history of interest rates to learn what their consistent rates turn out to be.

Central Bank

Central banks are national monetary authorities or reserve banks that are given the unique privilege and responsibility of loaning a government its currency. Central banks have many of the same characteristics that traditional banks do, such as charging set rates of interest on loans that they make to borrowers like the government of the country that they represent, or alternatively to commercial banks in dire need and as a last resort.

Central banks are different from regular banks in a variety of interest ways. Chief among these is their monopoly of creating the nation's currency. They also have the power to loan such currency out to their government as fully legal tender. These banks are the only ones that will lend to commercial banks in difficult times of need, too.

The main role of a central bank is to issue and oversee a country's supply of money. Besides this, they also engage in a number of more vigorous activities including setting and monitoring the interest rates of subsidized loans and helping out the banking sector in periods of financial difficulties or even crisis. Some central banks additionally supervise the commercial banking sector and individual banks in order to make certain that they do not engage in corrupt behavior or rash decision making and practices.

Not all countries possess central banks that are independent of the other branches of government's meddling and interference. Most of the wealthy countries of the world do have this type of central bank in a system that stops politicians from intervening in monetary policy. The European Central Bank, Bank of England, and Federal Reserve System of the United States are all good examples of independent central banks. Central banks can be privately held or publicly owned. In the U.S., the Federal Reserve proves to be a unique combination of private and public components.

Central banks are involved in many important functions. These include carrying out monetary policy and fixing the nation's interest rates. They also control their country's whole money supply. They act as both banker for the government and for all of a country's banks in difficult times. Central banks similarly handle the nation's gold reserves and foreign exchange reserves.

They may adjust these by buying or selling more gold, or by balancing the amount and kinds of currencies that they hold at any time. Many central banks supervise their banking industries as well, though not all perform this function. Central banks also help to deal with and combat inflation and manage a country's currency exchange rate by modifying the nation's official interest rates and utilizing similar policies to ensure that the desired outcomes of low inflation and stable currency exchange rates are in fact achieved.

Certificate of Deposit (CD)

A Certificate of Deposit refers to a kind of savings vehicle which generally provides greater returns for money invested than the typical savings accounts do. There is very little risk in such an account. They also come without monthly fees. Besides this, these CDs prove to be significantly different from the age old savings accounts for several reasons.

Such a Certificate of Deposit stands for a time deposit. While an individual who has a savings account is freely able to make additional deposits or withdraw available funds relatively at will, this is not the case with CDs. Holders of CDs consent to tying up their money for a minimum length of time. Banks calls this the term length. Such term lengths might be only a few days. They could also extend up to ten years out. Standard CD's run from typically three months to five years.

In general, the longer the term length proves to be, the better the rate of interest the Certificate of Deposit will pay. The longer the term length is, the greater amount of time an individual ties up the money in the account at the bank too. It makes sense that the bank rewards customers for committing to a longer amount of time with a larger CD rate than they pay on comparable savings accounts.

Banks generally quote these CD rates using the APY annual percentage yield. This rate takes into account the compounding periods on how often the CD pays interest which can then earn still more interest on it. The banks have the choice of compounding periods based on annually, quarterly, monthly, and daily compounding. The closer a CD compounds to a daily rate, the higher the APY will actually prove to be.

There are penalties involved with drawing the money out of the certificate of deposit before its final maturity date. While every bank is different, most banks will levy a penalty of from three to six months in accrued interest for breaking the time deposit early. This is why financial professionals will counsel against taking money out of a CD early unless it is desperately important to access the funds.

The U.S. FDIC Federal Deposit Insurance Corporation backs the CDs at the overwhelming majority of commercial banks in the country. These

Certificates of Deposit are government guaranteed in amounts of up to $250,000. With the credit union CDs, these certificates become insured by the NCUA National Credit Union Administration for the same maximum amounts. Credit unions which are state-chartered will often utilize private insurance for their CDs. Not any of these forms of insurance cover the penalties for taking out the funds ahead of maturity. Such coverage comes automatically and does not have to be applied for in order for the time deposit to be insured.

There are several different varieties of Certificates of Deposit available. Variable rate CDs are those whose interest rate is connected to the prime interest rate, market indices, Treasury bills rates, or another underlying benchmark. They help depositors to gain from any future point interest rate increases. Callable CDs often include a better rate of interest than a traditional CD. The bank can unilaterally reduce the maturity term period on demand though.

No or low penalty CDs pay lower interest rates but allow investors to more easily obtain their money back from the time deposit without expensive penalties. They often require holders to keep a certain minimum balance in the CD. IRA CDs are traditional certificates of deposit which are contained within an IRA Individual Retirement Account. There are tax advantages and deferrals on taxes of interest payments with these. Finally, Jumbo CDs pay greater rates of interest in exchange for extremely high minimum balances of typically $100,000 and higher.

Commercial Banks

Commercial banks are those financial institutions which offer a wide range of financial services to a variety of clients. Chief among these services are issuing loans and receiving deposits. The customers of such commercial financial institutions are able to avail themselves of a broad range of investment products that such banks offer. Included in these are certificates of deposit and savings accounts. Such banks issue a wide variety of loans which range from car loans and business loans to home equity loans and mortgages.

Banks which are commercial in nature deliver a range of financial products like checking accounts, savings accounts, and certificates of deposit. Customers of banks prefer these kinds of financial products since they are guaranteed by the FDIC Federal Deposit Insurance Corporation within the U.S.

In consideration for their funds' deposit, the commercial banks provide interest to their clients against their deposits. This is how these institutions realize profit--- they utilize the deposits of their customers to make loans that bring in higher interest rates than the ones they offer to their depositors. This spread from the amount the banks are paying out to the ones it is gathering back in becomes the net interest income of the commercial banks.

Such financial institutions do not all offer the same exact loan products to their various customers. They may specialize in several types or only a single kind of loan. These commercial banks are able to provide mortgages to purchase homes and home equity loans. In these cases, the houses provide the collateral to underlie the loans. Such financial institutions also provide auto loans with the vehicles as the loan collateral. The institutions similarly deliver personal loans, credit cards, and lines of credit to well-qualified borrowers.

Besides the interest such banks earn for their loans on the books, they can also create income through levying fees on their customers for banking services. This is common on products including checking and savings accounts, credit cards, and especially mortgage applications and originations.

There has been an evolution within the universe of commercial banks over the last two decades. Institutions that originally began as traditionally physical "brick and mortar" outlets complete with bank tellers, ATM's, bank vaults, and safe deposit boxes are still dominant. Yet a new and powerful challenger has arisen. This is the story of the commercial bank without physical branch locations.

Such virtual banks, or online only banks, lack physical branches. They force customers to do all of their transactions either over the Internet or by phone banking. The trade off for this accommodation is that these financial institutions deliver higher interest rates for accounts, deposits, and investments as their overheads are substantially lower. They also tend to charge significantly smaller and fewer fees. They can do this since they lack all of the associated costs which come with property taxes, rents, utilities, and additional staff salaries and benefits.

It is important to realize that the activities of commercial banking are vastly different than those of their colleagues in investment banking. With investment banking, the institutions engage in a number of stock and financial markets-related businesses. Among these are financial markets underwriting, performing tasks as intermediaries between the investors of and issuers of securities, fostering and participating in mergers and acquisitions and various kinds of corporate restructurings, and performing services as primary broker on behalf of institutional clients.

Other commercial banks boast investment banking divisions. This means that they are both involved in commercial banking and investment banking all at once. These include such well-known and enormous American financial institutions as JPMorgan Chase and Citibank and the multinational giant British banks like HSBC and Barclays. Other operations including Ally focus exclusively on the commercial banking segment of the industry.

Commodity Money

There are several forms of money which have been used throughout history. The oldest and best proven form is known as commodity money. A form of money invented in the past century which has become the major competitor to this historical currency is called fiat money. A newer post-modern technologically advanced form of spending power is today's electronic money. All three have their pros and cons, yet the arguments about commodities being safe and trusted keep them alive despite their critics colorfully referring to them as barbaric relics of ancient history.

Commodity money is that type of money that possesses intrinsic value on its own, independent of any governing body. This means the money itself contains its own worth. It is not merely a token or representative of financial value as with bank notes or numbers on a computer screen and in a ledger. The longest reigning and best loved form of commodity money remains gold and silver coins. Their history is legendary and stretches back five thousand years through times good, bad, and tragic.

Any type of commodity is able to fulfill the role of commodity money. As long as the money's value springs from the material from which it is comprised and not some arbitrary decree of a ruler or government representative, it is in fact hard money. Numerous commodities in various times and places have been effectively utilized as this form of tired and true currency. Besides gold and silver, peoples, nations, and empires have employed salt, chocolate beans, copper, decorative belts, shells, cigarettes, and even large stones. Critics have argued that many of these forms of currency were prone to spoilage or gradual deterioration.

The overwhelming majority of cash forms with which people buy and sell nowadays lack any intrinsic value whatsoever. Banknotes are a case in point. They are fiat money. This is money that only contains any value because the government decrees it has the full faith and credit of the nation backing it. It works because members of society and businesses choose to accept it as their primary form of currency and means of exchanging goods and services.

It is interesting that commodity money does not have to be inherently useful to the owner to have value for exchange. Few people have practical uses for gold or silver coins. These coins have dramatically high value because goldsmiths and jewelers are able to utilize them to produce costly jewelry or collectible items of great worth and because of their inherent scarcity.

When societies choose to utilize such commodity money as metal coins for their official legal tender, it is up to the government in question to determine the fixed value of each coin in the currency lineup. The face value of these coins is the one that will be accepted rather than the value of the metal contained within each piece.

Coins are usually circulated at a face value that is greater than the costs of the underlying metal materials. There are some cases, as with runaway inflation, where coins can have greater metal value than face value. This is especially the case with coins made mostly or entirely from gold or silver. When this is a persistent problem, governments often attack the problem by taking that currency unit out of circulation.

Fiat money is the opposite of this commodity money. Fiat money only derives its value from legal claims and obligations of the law. It is truly like a purchase voucher which can be utilized to exchange for services and goods. This means that its purchasing power varies. Fiat money only has fixed value in settling debts. Originally it emerged as a means of convenience so that individuals could carry lighter paper certificates that the government guaranteed rather than having to ship and guard heavy gold and silver.

Over time, governments stealthily stopped exchanging this paper money for the gold and silver that originally backed it. Fiat money is now useless intrinsically and can not be redeemed for any commodity as it once could. The only reason it has any value at all is because the government says it will be valued for that purpose.

Credit Agricole

Credit Agricole calls itself the foremost financial partner in the French economy. This is not idle boasting as they have a number of impressive accolades to their credit. It is rated the second largest bank in France and third largest banking group in Europe by assets. What makes it different from other global banks is that it proves to be a cooperative and mutual organization rather than a standard commercial bank.

The Credit Agricole group counts 140,000 employees working under the leadership of 31,500 directors in its regional and local banks. The bank serves 52 million individual and business customers and has 8.2 million mutual share holders. There are also 1.1 million traditional individual share holders.

By some measures, this banking group is the most important bank on the continent. It turns out to be the foremost retail bank in Europe by branch numbers and the largest manager of European assets. The group is the leading bank assurer in the continent and the third biggest player in the world of project financing.

The group operates under the universal retail bank model. The individual retail banks cooperate together under a unique arrangement. Their regional banks are independent banks in which the corporate Credit Agricole owns 25% stakes. They work together on the common business lines. Besides retail banking, these include real estate, insurance, asset management, payments, consume finance, leasing and factoring, and investment and corporate banking. The group is listed on the stock exchange Euronext in Paris.

The group provides finance and technical assistance for not only customer projects found in France, but also throughout the world. Credit Agricole has locations in more than 37 countries and territories around the globe. The bank corporation operates with a central body, a central bank, and an entity which handles the group's strategic development. The entity provides coordination to the numerous business lines in France and internationally. They ensure that the bank runs smoothly and cohesively despite the independent nature of the regional banks.

The banking group operates in three lines of business. These are French and international retail banking, specialized business lines, and corporate & investment banking.

Credit Agricole has 2,512 local banks that are the basis of the banking group. These local banks own the majority of the capital of the Regional Banks. The other 25% is owned by the corporation. There are over 6.9 million members who own the local banks. The group's 39 regional banks provide services to farmers, individuals, corporations, businesses, and local governments. In daily banking services, this group is the leading French bank.

The regional banks provide a wide range of services. This includes investments, savings, loans, life insurance, property/casualty insurance, and payment instruments. They boast 20 million customers and hold the rank of number one in practically every local market in France. These regional banks also own the majority stake position in the Credit Agricole corporation as a whole. Regional banks obtain information, express opinions, and engage in dialogue with each other through the FNCA Fédération Nationale du Crédit Agricole.

Credit Agricole's main rivals in France include BNP Paribas, Societe Generale, and Group BPCE. These other competing banks are more traditional commercial banks that are not majority owned by their members as cooperatives or mutual organizations. This has not helped any of them to become larger by assets except for BNP Paribas.

Credit Bureaus

Credit bureaus are agencies that collect financial information. They go by different names in various countries around the world. In the United Kingdom they are known as credit reference agencies. In Australia, the bureaus are called credit reporting bodies. India knows their credit agencies as credit information companies.

Within the United States, these organizations are called consumer reporting agencies. Whatever name they go by, they all serve the same function. The bureaus gather information from banks and other financial sources to deliver consumer credit information about individual consumers.

The U.S. consumer reporting agencies are governed by the Fair Credit Reporting Act. Other laws that regulate the activities of the bureaus are the Fair and Accurate Credit Transactions Act, the Fair Credit Billing Act, the Fair Credit Reporting Act, and Regulation B. These acts attempt to safeguard consumers against unfair practices and mistakes made by the data providers and the credit reporting agencies themselves.

The U.S. has two separate government organizations who oversee the credit bureaus and their data suppliers. These are the FTC and the OCC. Primary oversight of the credit reporting agencies as they deal with consumers belongs to the Federal Trade Commission. The banks are monitored for all of the information that they provide the reporting agencies by the Office of the Controller of the Currency. This government agency supervises, regulates, and charters all of the national banks and any information they turn over to the consumer credit reporting agencies.

Three main credit reporting bureaus dominate nearly all credit reporting in the U.S. These are Experian, Equifax, and TransUnion. None of these three agencies are owned by government entities. All of them exist as companies seeking to make a profit and are traded publically. They are carefully monitored for fairness by the government provided oversight organizations.

The consumer reporting agencies operate through a vast network with the credit card issuing companies, banks, and other financial entities with which individuals have accounts. All of these ties ensure that credit account information and histories show up on the credit reports of one, two, or even all of the bureaus.

The credit bureaus compile all of this information into a consumer credit report. They each then utilize proprietary trade secret formulas to determine every individual's FICO credit score. Each of the three bureaus formulates its own score that is different from that of its competitors. They also come up with educational credit score numbers which are often vastly different from the official scores.

Consumers do not have to settle for educational credit scores. They have the rights to see what is on their credit reports. Each and every year, individuals are able to obtain an official credit report from each of the three credit bureaus. This can be done by going to the government mandated website AnnualCreditReport.com.

Besides this, consumers are allowed to go to the websites of the three main consumer reporting agencies and order credit reports and scores from them directly. The only way to get the official credit score is to pay for and order it from the credit bureaus themselves. These are not provided in the annual free reports. Experian and Equifax offer all three credit reports in a single convenient to view document.

Sometimes the credit bureaus will make mistakes with individuals' credit reports. When this happens, it is important to get in touch with the credit bureau itself in order to dispute any information that is inaccurate. These organizations also should be contacted directly if there is concern about fraud so that they can place a security alert or fraud alert on the person's credit report.

Credit Repair Organizations

Credit repair organizations are those which offer to assist individuals with clearing up their credit report and improving their credit scores. While a number of them are legitimate operations, others can be scams. Such credit repair clinics often charge exorbitant prices to perform services that individuals can do for themselves. There were enough problems with fraud or unfulfilled promises from these organizations that Congress created a law to reduce abuse. This is known as the Credit Repair Organizations Act.

Many credit repair organizations will offer to have incorrect information removed from the credit file of an individual. Consumers can do this themselves according to the provisions of the Fair Credit Reporting Act. Others will promise to take off information that is negative but correct from the files. Generally this takes seven years or longer for such information to go away if it is accurate.

The credit repair clinics have a strategy to challenge all items in a customer's file. These could be neutral, negative, or positive. They do this hoping that they can overwhelm the credit bureaus so that they will simply take off information rather than verify it first. The problem with this tactic is that credit bureaus are allowed under the Fair Credit Reporting Act to dismiss frivolous challenges. There are cases where the credit bureau may remove such information. The problem is that correct information often shows up again in one to two months as the original creditors will report negative information again.

Credit repair organizations also offer to have court judgments and existing debt balances taken off of credit files. They can do this by negotiating partial or whole payments with the creditors in exchange for taking negative information away from the credit report. While these are legitimate negotiation tactics, individuals can do this without having to pay credit repair clinics for the service.

Another suggestion that such credit repair organizations may make to consumer clients is to obtain a secured credit card from a bank which offers them. These are simply credit cards that individuals use after putting a deposit in an account at their bank. These secured credit card lists that the credit repair clinics offer are not proprietary. Individuals can find the same information for free or very little online.

Congress attempted to curb abuses from credit repair clinics with their Credit Repair Organizations Act. It regulates these clinics that are for profit. The law states that these credit repair outfits must provide individuals with written statements of rights provided by the FCR Act. They must correctly present what they are and are not able to accomplish. They are not allowed to charge and collect fees until they render all services which they promised.

The credit repair clinic must provide a contract in writing. They have to allow consumers to cancel the contracts within three days of signing them. Consumers must provide such cancellations in writing. All contracts that do not follow the Credit Repair Organizations Act become void. Consumers can not sign away any of their rights.

There are unethical credit repair clinics which have found a means to get around the law. They incorporate themselves as not for profit organizations. This makes it easier for them to offer poor or limited results and to take customers' money. They also find it simpler to perform the same services that consumers can do for themselves this way.

Credit Union

A credit union represents a financial cooperative. Members own these financial institutions. It is these members who both start and run them so that they can reduce costs for financial services and share profits with each other.

There are a variety of sizes of these institutions. A credit union might be a small operation that volunteers run. It could also be a substantial outfit with thousands of members or more. The idea is the same in either case. The business model has members pooling their savings within the credit union so that they can make loans to other members and receive financial benefits. Such benefits include lower interest rates on loans and higher savings rates.

Credit unions are similar to building societies in Britain, Australia, and other countries. Many of the building societies that allow members to invest their money to help members buy or build houses were started in the 1800's. Halifax in the United Kingdom is the largest in the world with 18 million members.

It is easy to become a member of a credit union, especially when individuals are invited. Once they deposit initial funds into the account at the institution, they become part owners of the organization. This allows them to share in the profits that it makes. They also gain the rights to vote for the board of directors of the credit union and in other important decisions.

Many credit unions get started because a large corporation or other organization wants to offer these benefits to their employers or their members. In cases like these, profits can be invested in community services, membership interests, or projects that benefit the members. Credit unions are considered not for profit. This is because they are helping the community or their members out rather than making a profit for the organization itself.

When credit unions began in America, the membership had limitations to those who held a common bond with others in the group. They might have to live in the same town or work in the industry of the other members. Credit unions have since loosened up the rules for becoming a member. Banks have been frustrated by this development that permits many people to participate in a rival organization which does not have to pay taxes.

There are some risks to belonging to this type of organization. If the union is unable to cover its expenses beyond the services, they could possibly fail. Should the organization not possess enough cash flow, it will be unable to run the operations smoothly enough to take care of the members. At this point, it would be closed.

The benefits of belonging to such an organization are significant. The friendliness and feeling of community is greater than from an average bank. The unions also give benefits that a bank will not, like less expensive loans, better rates for credit, and other financial services without fees or with lower costs. Other unions provide the membership with significant advantages like free insurance coverage or reduced cost and free education.

The building societies of Europe predated credit unions in America. The first ones in the U.S. appeared in the 1900s. St. Mary's Bank Credit Union of Manchester, New Hampshire became the first such organization in America. They are now found all over the globe. Some of them in the U.S. now run under the regulations of the Federal government instead of state regulations.

Custodian Bank

A custodian bank is a special financial institution that carries the responsibility for protecting the financial assets of individuals or companies. These institutions can also be called simply custodians. Such outfits serve as a third party check that protects the assets they are guarding against the fund managers and any illegal activities they may pursue.

Congress established these custodian banks with the Investment Company Act of 1940 in order to protect investors. Thanks to this particular legislation, investment companies must adhere to specific stringent listing requirements and must be registered with the Securities and Exchange Commission.

The custodian bank performs a number of activities in their primary function of watching over the financial assets of businesses and individuals. They settle sales and purchases of bonds and equities and physically protect the certificates of these assets. These institutions also gather information about and income from such assets. When the assets are stocks this means dividends. When the instruments are bonds, they collect the interest from the coupons. The custodians also disperse information they gather, pertaining to yearly general meetings and shareholder voting. They handle any foreign exchange transfers as necessary and manage all cash transactions. Finally, custodians deliver routine reports on their various activities to the customers.

Custodians banks provide reports on every trade or deal which they transact on behalf of the clients. They must be consistently delivered. Along with these reports they furnish information on the companies whose assets they hold besides information on general meetings. When a custodian is holding foreign shares or bonds, they will also have to change currencies as necessary. This is the case when the fund manager buys or sells foreign currency assets. It is also necessary when companies pay out dividends or bonds receive interest with these overseas financial instruments. Custodian banks are a critical component of the modern investment environment. Without them to carry out these functions, all of the important financial record keeping and housekeeping items would be neglected.

Not all custodian banks are national operations in the United States. A number of the major international financial institutions offer these services around the globe. These are called global custodians. Such international outfits use their own branches in the various countries in which they operate to manage the accounts and assets for their customers. In other cases, they may employ other custodians to assist them with these services. In these types of situations, the customer assets will be held by pension funds.

There are also local custodian banks whose job is to handle the ADR American Depository Receipts. These stock certificates are from foreign based companies that wish to offer their securities to the American stock markets. There are a number of international and large national American banks that participate as these local custodians. Among them are BNP Paribas, PFPC (a subsidiary of PNC Financial Services Group), Brown Brothers Harriman and Company, Kaupthing Bank, Citigroup, Northern Trust, Credit Suisse, RBC Dexia, Societe Generale, State Street Corp., German Bank AG, Goldman Sachs, HSBC, The Bank of New York Mellon, UBS AG, Union Bank of California, JPMorgan Chase Bank, and TD Bank NV.

Debit Card

Debit cards are plastic cards that function like a check and are easily utilized like a credit card. Debit cards are commonly one of two types, either branded Visa or Master Card. When you use such a debit card to pay for a purchase, then this amount is deducted immediately from your checking account. Both convenience and security features are included in the use of a debit card.

Debit cards provide tremendous convenience in their ease of use. No longer do you have to make sure that you are carrying enough money on you, or to take the time to write out a physical check while the long line waits impatiently behind you. Besides this ease of use, debit cards are accepted at literally millions of places around the country and the world.

Nowadays, they can be used for almost any purchase, such as lunches or dinners at restaurants, monthly bill payments, merchandise in retail stores, groceries, prescriptions, gas, online purchases, over the phone orders, and even fast food.

Debit cards' spending is easy to keep track of as well. The majority of such transactions are both deducted and posted to a checking account in twenty-four hours or less. This allows for you to conveniently monitor your constantly updated transaction record and balance either over the phone or the bank or card issuer's website. Besides this, debit cards also offer statements, much like credit cards, that outline all purchases made, with details on the name of the merchant, date, location, and amount of transaction.

Debit cards offer another benefit in their security provisions. These cards include free fraud monitoring that helps to find and stop activity that is suspicious with your debit card. They also come with policies of zero liability that protect you from charges that you did not make or authorize. Fraudulently taken out funds are guaranteed to be returned to your account. The vast majority of debit cards also come with the security feature of three digit security codes that allow you to confirm your identity for both phone and Internet orders and purchases.

Debit cards allow two ways for completing in person transactions. One of these is through swiping the card and then signing the receipt issued by the merchant representative. The other is via using a pad with your PIN, or personal identification code, after the card is swiped.

A final benefit that you gain from a debit card is that most of them provide rewards that are earned simply by utilizing them. These are earned in one of two ways. With Visa Debit cards, you are able to receive discounts from some merchants who provide these special price breaks for the holders of Visa cards.

Other debit cards provide extras rewards programs. These rewards programs pay you back with some type of reward for every purchase that you make. These can be cash rebates or more commonly awards that are earned through the collection of such points.

Debt Service

Debt service refers to the cash that is necessary to be paid over a certain period of time in order to repay both principal and interest on a given debt. For individuals, monthly mortgage payments, or credit card bill payments, prove to be good examples of personal debt service. For businesses, payments on lines of credit, business loans, or coupon payments of bonds represent samples of corporate debt service.

Where businesses or personal debt service is concerned, this is used to calculate the DSCR, or debt service coverage ratio. This ratio is that of the cash that is on hand for servicing the debt's principal, interest, and lease payments. This measurement is a much utilized benchmark that helps to determine a company or an individual's capability of generating sufficient money to cover the payments on their debt. With a higher debt service coverage ratio, loans are easier to get for both companies and people.

The commercial banking industry also employs this phrase. Here, it can refer to the minimally acceptable ratio that a given lender will accept. This might turn out to be a condition of making the entity such a loan in the end. When this type of a condition is part of the loan covenant, then violating the debt service coverage ratio can sometimes be considered an action of default.

Debt service coverage ratios are similarly used in the world of corporate finance. Here, they describe the sum of available cash flow that is usable for covering yearly principal and interest payments on any and all debts. This includes payments for sinking funds.

Commercial real estate finance similarly utilizes debt service and debt service coverage ratios as the main means of discovering if a given property is capable of maintaining its level of debt using only its own cash flow. In the past ten or so years, banks would look for a minimum debt service coverage ratio of minimally 1.2. Banks that proved to be more aggressive were willing to work with lower ratios.

This practice led to greater risk in the system that helped to bring on the financial meltdown and resulting crisis that stretched from 2007 to 2010. When an entity has more than a ratio of one debt service coverage ratio, it is theoretically capable of covering its debt requirements with cash flow. Similarly, if this ratio is less than one, then the statistics claim that an insufficient amount of cash flow exists to meet the required loan payments.

Discover

Discover Financial Services turns out to be a United States' based global financial service outfit. They issue and service the Discover Card and Diners Club International Card and operate Pulse Networks. Their flagship card proves to be the third biggest brand of credit cards within the U.S. based on the number of cards in use. The company boasts almost 50 million different card holders nationally.

Sears began the Discover legacy by introducing the card originally back in 1985. It launched the original credit card with cash rewards a year later in 1986. Stock broker Dean Witter acquired the card from Sears and then later merged its company with Morgan Stanley in 1997. The Discover Financial Services first acquired its independence with the spin off of the company in 2007. It became a publicly traded corporation headquartered in Riverwoods, Illinois, a Chicago suburb.

The company is involved with both credit cards and banking. This business offers their proprietary brand credit cards, personal loans, private student loans, checking and savings accounts, home equity loans, money market accounts, and certificates of deposit to its clients.

Their customers include both consumers and small businesses today who utilize their travel, cash, and gift cards throughout the U.S. and the world. Their two banking affiliates are Bank of New Castle and Discover Bank. Both are regulated and chartered through the FDIC and the Office of the Delaware State Bank Commissioner. The FDIC is both their insurer and federal regulator.

Besides being among the largest credit card issuers in the country and a significant bank, the company also owns and operates the PULSE network. This is a national leading network of ATM/debit machines. For more than three decades they have provided this among the largest in the country networks.

It offers services to over 4,500 credit unions, banks, and other financial institutions throughout the United States. Cardholders are linked up with POS payment terminals and ATM machines around the U.S. through their services. PULSE is technologically advanced in its offering of simultaneous transaction processing and settlement.

They also own Diners Club International since 2008. This globally known brand provides financial payment services and credit for small businesses, corporations, and consumers. Launched in 1950, Diners Club International provided the world's original multiple use credit cards. Its cards boast acceptance in over 185 countries via millions of cash access points and merchant locations across the globe today.

Thanks to these combined operations, literally billions of different financial transactions go through their network of electronic payments every year. The Discover Network handles a complete line up of cards, including prepaid, debit, and credit cards. Their programs and tools were created to assist merchants, acquirers, and issues in growing their transactional volumes and operating their payment processing needs with effective and efficient operations. Internationally, the network relies on two different alliances that help to ensure the card is well accepted overseas. China UnionPay and JCB offer and receive reciprocal card acceptance throughout numerous nations around the globe.

Discover prides itself on its long running customer satisfaction success. For three years in a row through 2016, it has been ranked the "Highest in Customer Satisfaction with Credit Card Companies" by J.D. Power.

Exchange Rate

In finance and business, exchange rates are also known as Forex Rates, foreign exchange rates, or FX rates. These exchange rates are the rates that are valid between two currencies. They are stated in terms of one currency's value in the other currency. Such an exchange rate is also the foreign nation's currency value as stated in the currency of the home nation.

There are various distinctions within the category of exchange rates. Present day exchange rates are termed spot exchange rates. Exchange rates which are quoted to you and traded today but available for payment and delivery in the future on a particular date are called forward exchange rates.

It is instructive to look at some examples. If the GBP/USD rate is 1.60, then it means that the exchange rate of the British Pound garners $1.60 in US dollars. Alternatively, a USD/CHF rate of .97 would mean that only .97 of a Swiss Franc will buy one U.S. dollar.

Exchange rates are determined on the foreign exchange market. This is the largest single market on the whole planet, trading literally trillions of dollars in currency values every single day. It is estimated that this market exceeds three trillion dollars in U.S. valued currencies on a given trading day. This market trades six days a week, and is only closed from Friday at 5PM New York time until Sunday afternoon at 3PM New York Time.

Exchange rates can be freely trading on the world exchange markets. Some countries choose to instead peg the value of their currency to another proven, more responsible, and reliable currency, such as the Euro or the dollar. In these cases, the exchange rates are constant against those that they peg to, and only fluctuate against other currencies on the market at the same pace as the currency that they are pegged to does.

Exchange rates on FOREX can be pursued for hedging purposes or for investment opportunities. Businesses that have operations in two or more countries are often interested in locking in their exchange rate in order to protect themselves from possibly violent currency swings. By buying forward exchange rates, they can lock these in for any given day that suits their needs. Alternatively, they can take on FOREX spot positions in the currency totals that they anticipate needing, so that as the price rises and falls, it will be canceled out as they repatriate their foreign currency back into home currency.

Investors can participate in the exchange rate markets for investment opportunities. Besides buying these spot currency positions or forward positions, they can purchase options contracts on these pairs. The advantage and disadvantage to these markets is the leverage that they provide, which is commonly one hundred to one. This signifies that an individual investor is able to control one hundred thousand Euros against the dollar with only a thousand dollar account value. Major gains, as well as substantial losses, become possible with only small moves, since every ten cent price change in this case represents a hundred dollars literally gained or lost.

Federal Reserve System

The Federal Reserve System is the United States' central banking system. It is made up of the Federal Open Market Committee, the Federal Reserve Board, 12 regional Federal Reserve Banks, and state and national member banks.

Seven members make up the Board of Governors. These the President appoints to 14 year terms upon approval by the Senate. The reason this system became established was to manage the movement of credit and money in the U.S. Congress set up this system in 1913. The U.S. had experienced a variety of central banks since 1791. The country needed a more stable banking system to help encourage a stronger economy.

Practically every bank in the U.S. participates in the Federal Reserve System. The program requires these institutions to keep a set amount of their assets deposited with their area Federal Reserve Bank. The Board of Governors determines how much these reserve requirements will be. The Board of Governors changes these required reserves in order to significantly influence the money supply that is circulating in the economy.

This Federal Reserve System provides a few different functions to the country. It is a bank for all the banks. A great number of interbank transactions go through this system. Banks may also borrow money from the Federal Reserve if they can not get credit from anywhere else. The system only gives them credit in emergencies or as it is unavailable on the open markets.

The Federal Reserve also functions like the bank of the government. The inbound and outbound payments of the tax system process via a checking account at the bank. The Fed further supplies the currency of the United States even though they do not produce it. They also purchase and sell government securities like Treasury Bills and Bonds.

Among the more important functions of this system is its purpose as a regulatory agency. They act as policeman to the banking sector to protect consumers' rights and to ensure smooth functions. They are also the main resource for banks and the public in times of financial crises or a panic surrounding the banks.

National banks have to be members of the system. In order to qualify, they are made to deposit the reserve requirements from their customer checking and savings accounts in their regional Federal Reserve bank. They must also keep mandatory reserve levels with this bank. Every nationally chartered bank has to be a member of the system. State chartered banks are also encouraged to join as members of the system.

The need for this Federal Reserve System became apparent after several failed attempts at establishing a uniform banking system in the United States. The first central bank was the First Bank that existed from 1791 to 1811. The Second Bank took over this role from 1816 to 1836. These two outfits proved to be the U.S. Treasury Department's only official representatives. This meant that they were the only organizations issuing and promoting the official U.S. currency.

Every other bank in the country ran under private auspices or as a state chartered organization. Each bank had its own bank notes which competed against the two U.S. banks as currency that could be redeemed for face value.

The first National Bank Act that Congress passed in 1863 allowed for a regimen of National Banks that would be supervised. Banks had to abide by certain operating practices, rules for making and issuing loans, and capital amount minimums kept in the banks. The Act effectively killed the non national individual bank currencies by creating a 10% tax on all state level banknotes.

Fedwire

Fedwire represents an RTGS, or real time gross settlement system. This settling system pertains to central and commercial bank funds which are utilized within the United States. The Federal Reserve Banks employ it to electronically settle all of their final payments between the various member institutions. All final payment settlement is performed exclusively within U.S. dollars.

Fedwire is actually operated and owned by all 12 of the American Federal Reserve Banks. This networked system of payments and electronic processing works exclusively between the member of the Federal Reserve system banks and the regional 12 Reserve Banks. The participants in the system, which are Fedwire member banks, can also use it between each other as well.

Fedwire members include two groups. The first of these are the financial institutions of the U.S. which are depository banks. Besides this, American branches of many approved foreign financial institutions and also allowed government groups are members. They must keep an active account with one of the Federal Reserve Banks to maintain their membership as either foreign or domestic entities.

The actual Fedwire system has been newly designed in recent years. Now this national clearing system works in high technology and automated real time for all of the businesses which are involved in the Federal Reserve financial network. This includes nearly 10,000 banks. The system allows a single bank to wire funds over to a fellow domestic bank practically instantly. The Federal Reserve has its own uses for the system of course. They deploy its cutting-edged technology in order to ascertain credit. They also orchestrate the effective movement of capital throughout the nation with it.

Many people think of the Federal Reserve as a branch of the U.S. government, yet this is not truly the case. It is a private company which delivers the centralized banking system to the United States. As the directors and board members are appointed by the President though, this makes it more like a GSE government sponsored enterprise. Many critics have complained about the private nature of the United States central bank over the years. The ones who are closest to it refute these objections by declaring it to be a one of a kind mixture that is at once private and public administration which no single private entity owns and controls.

The 12 regional Federal Reserve Banks serve a vital function for the nation in helping to oversee and implement the financial policy of America. All of the commercial banks which are federally chartered financial institutions are required to hold stock in the various Federal Reserve banks.

Thanks to the new Fedwire setup, banks can count on a true real time gross settlement of their funding transfers. It means that the automated financial transfers are not only seamless, but they complete rapidly. There are many effective uses to the impressive system.

Financial institutions are able to effect payments to the SEC Securities Exchange Commission using it. Since banks and other financial institutions have to regularly remit fees to the SEC for its oversight of Wall Street and the stock market, this is a convenient means of transferring payments to them. Many of the banks choose to use the system for just such a purpose.

The member banks utilize various protocols and "tags" to ensure that they are creating standard transactions on the electronic network. Part of what makes this system so technologically advanced is it even searches out problems in resulting syntax which might delay a transaction between member banks or with the 12 regional Federal Reserve Banks in the system.

This electronic funds settling system of the Federal Reserve proves to be much like those deployed in other nations around the world. A number of countries already had their own financial networks like this. Still others are in the process of being created, designed, and developed. Such financial settlement systems drag antiquated financial regimes into the current century. This is appropriate since a huge amount of wealth and cash are already handled by automated and digital electronic systems and technologies worldwide.

Fixed Rate Mortgage

Fixed Rate Mortgages are products for mortgage loans that the FHA, or Federal Housing Administration, first created. In this type of mortgage, the interest rates in effect on the mortgage note stay at the same level during the entire life of the loan. This stands in stark contrast to loans where the interest rates are adjustable, or floating. There are also hybrid types of loans that involve fixed rates for a portion of the loan's life.

Fixed rate mortgages will have monthly payments that must be made to keep current on the mortgage. Besides the monthly payment there are property taxes and property insurance costs. These are typically set up in escrow accounts. With such escrow amounts, these are likely to change every so often. Still, the main share of the payments, which are associated with interest and principal on the mortgage, will stay the same.

Figuring up the monthly payments with fixed rate mortgages is relatively easy. You will have to acquire three pieces of data to do so. These are the interest rate with compounding of interest period, mortgage term, and amount of loan.

Fixed rate mortgages are also known by their nickname of plain vanilla mortgages. They have this moniker because of how simple they are for borrowers to understand. Such fixed rate mortgages do not entail the many risks and perils associated with adjustable rate mortgages that include pre set teasing rates or Adjustable Rate Mortgages. As such, Fixed rate mortgage default rates and foreclosure rates are commonly far lower than are these more experimental and risky mortgage products.

Several terms are commonly associated with Fixed Rate Mortgages. These include the fully indexed rate and the term. Fully indexed rates are the interest rate index plus the margin charged by the lender. Such a fully indexed rate proves to be the actual interest rate for the loan's entire life.

The term represents the amount of time that the fixed rate loan covers. This is not the same thing as the number of payments. Thirty year terms might have thirty payments if you were on an annual payment plan, or it might alternatively have 360 payments on a more usual monthly payment plan

The most popular and proven form of home loans and mortgage products within the United States are undoubtedly these fixed rate mortgages. Among the various mortgage terms that can be acquired, the most prevalent ones are either thirty year or fifteen year mortgages. Both shorter and longer time frames can be had with fixed rate mortgages.

These days, even forty and fifty year mortgages are presently offered. They are especially utilized in places with housing prices that are exceptionally high, as thirty year mortgage terms do not prove to be affordable for the average income family in such scenarios.

In contrast to fixed rate mortgages are various other types. These include graduated payment mortgages, balloon payment mortgages, and interest only mortgages. These unusual other types of mortgages commonly get borrowers into trouble, which is why they are not nearly so popular as are the fixed rate mortgages.

Government Sponsored Enterprise (GSE)

A government sponsored enterprise is a financial service operations that the U.S. Congress created by law. Their purpose is to improve the amount of credit that flows into specific areas of the American economy. They were also intended to help those parts of the capital markets become more transparent and efficient as well as to lessen risks for investors and capital suppliers.

The wish of Congress in establishing them was to increase the available finance and lower the cost of obtaining it for certain specific segments of the economy. This was to be accomplished by encouraging investors via lowering the risks of losses to those involved.

The main components of the economy where these were set up were home finance, agriculture, and education. Among these, two of the government sponsored enterprises are best known. These are Fannie Mae, the Federal National Mortgage Association and Freddie Mac, the Federal Home Loan Mortgage Corporation.

The year 1916 saw the first government sponsored enterprise that Congress established. This was the Farm Credit System. Congress moved GSEs into housing finance in 1932 when it established the Federal Home Loan Banks. It focused on education costs and finance when in 1972 Congress chartered Sallie Mae. In 1995, Congress passed a law and permitted this educational GSE to give up its government sponsorship so that it could transform into a fully private company.

The segment of the economy for residential mortgages and borrowing proves to be substantially the largest industry where the government sponsored enterprises function. In mortgages, these GSEs own or pool around $5 trillion in home mortgages.

The way that Congress came up with to boost capital market efficiency and get past the imperfections of the market was to help funds migrate more effortlessly from fund suppliers to fund borrowers in major loan demand areas of the economy. They accomplished this with a type of government guarantee which limited the loss risks for those who offered the funds.

These government sponsored enterprises now mostly serve as intermediaries between agricultural and home borrowers and lenders. Freddie Mac and Fannie Mae remain the two best known and most influential GSEs today. They buy up mortgages and issue them through affiliated companies. Once this is accomplished, they pack them up as MBS mortgage backed securities. These securities come with the important financial backing from Freddie Mac or Fannie Mae. Investors allowed to trade in the TBA to be announced markets find these investments appealing when they carry government sponsored enterprises backing.

These housing GSEs also established a secondary market for loans with their guarantees, securitizing, and bonding. It has helped the main issuers of primary market mortgages to boost their volume of loans at the same time as they reduce the risks of single loans. It also gives investors a wide market of instruments which are securitized and standardized.

The government sponsored enterprise does not actually come with the government's hard guarantee of their credit. Despite this, lenders have always given them better interest rates at the same time that investors in the securities have paid high prices. This stems from the government's implicit guarantee that these critical organizations will not default or fail. It has helped the two main GSEs to save on borrowing costs to the tune of around $2 billion each year.

The subprime mortgage crisis and financial crisis reached a fevered pitch and embroiled Freddie Mac and Fannie Mae in 2007 and 2008. The American government demonstrated the value of the implicit guarantee then by bailing out and putting the two GSEs into conservatorship in September of 2008.

Graduated Payment Mortgage (GPM)

A graduated payment mortgage is a special type of home mortgage where payments are low initially and go up over the term of the loan. These are still considered to be a type of fixed rate mortgages as the interest rates are set and pre-determined even when the payments rise.

The low upfront payment helps financial institutions to qualify the borrowers. Banks only have to take into account the original low rate to approve them. This is why the GPMs assist those who otherwise would not be able to get qualified using the normal FRM fixed rate mortgage. This aids a great number of potential home buyers who might not be able to get qualified to purchase a home. It is best for younger or newer homeowners. Their levels of income should rise with time. This helps them to make the increasing mortgage payments.

The payments rise every year with a graduated payment mortgage until the entire amount has been repaid. The amount that they increase varies from one contract to the next. Typically the payments rises between 7% and 12% each year from the original base amount.

There is a danger with these types of products. If the young home buyers do not see their income rise consistently and significantly enough, the increasing payments on the home will take a greater share of their take home pay every year. Eventually, they may not be able to afford the payments if their salaries do not rise sufficiently.

The original payment for these graduated payment mortgages is not enough to cover the loan's interest. The difference between what is covered and what is not is called negative amortization. This amount adds on to the loan balance with every payment. It takes years for the rising payments to overcome this increase in the loan balance. Lenders do not like the fact that the balance goes up above the initial amount. Because of this they charge greater rates for these types of loans than they do for standard fixed rate mortgages.

The trade-off with a graduated payment mortgage is the larger payment that continues to grow for several years. This generally does not reach its peak level until five years have passed. The higher payment will then stay fixed for the rest of the mortgage term. This is the price to pay for a low upfront payment that a borrower can be approved for and can afford.

There are other kinds of graduated payment mortgages on the market. These alternatives provide varying rates of payment rises for different amounts of time. In one example, homeowners can get a gradually rising rate of 3% per year for ten years rather than pay more than 7% each year for 5 years. These alternative GPMs require a higher upfront payment amount and can also lead to a larger final payment. Because the initial payment is higher, the negative amortization will be less. This will cause the peak loan balance to be smaller.

GPMs are not unique in mortgages that have payments which increase. There are also fixed rate mortgages called temporary buy downs. These come with lower upfront payments during the loan's early years. The advantage to these is that the loan does not incur negative amortization.

Temporary buy downs only work if someone pays for the buy down account. The financial institution takes money from this supplemental account to cover the lower payments in the first two years. This way the lender receives identical payments for the entire life of the loan. Either the home seller or the buyer has to supply the money for the supplemental account.

Halifax

The Halifax Building Society was a British bank based in the town of the same name in West Yorkshire, England. It was an independent British bank that became a trading division of the Bank of Scotland, which eventually became an entirely owned subsidiary of today's banking giant Lloyds Banking Group. Even as a subsidiary of a subsidiary, Halifax remains the biggest residential mortgages and savings accounts provider in the United Kingdom. In the 2016 British Bank Awards, it came in fifth in the overall rankings.

Halifax arose as a building society in the year 1853. These societies were organizations which allowed individuals with extra money to invest them in a pool for loaning out money to others who wished to buy or build a house. This particular building society grew into the biggest building society in all of the U.K. by 1913. From this point on, it only continued to expand and financially prosper. It held the number one lending position in Great Britain as an independent company through 1997 when the bank demutualized.

The early history of the Halifax Permanent Benefit Building and Investment Society allowed it to grow into the mortgage lending giant of the twentieth century. The idea became formulated at the Old Cock Inn in a meeting room above it close to where the first building of the Building Society would later be located. Local working people all benefited from the establishment of such a society. Those investors who had extra cash on hand could invest it in the society. They would receive interest payments. Borrowers were then able to apply for and receive loans to allow them to pay for buying a house.

Halifax Building Society did not expand through the typical mergers and acquisitions of other societies of the time. Instead, they grew organically. They began opening up branches all around the United Kingdom. They achieved the status of largest building society in Great Britain by 1913. They opened their first office in London by 1924 and the first locations in Scotland by 1928.

With the demutualization of 1997, the company evolved into a public limited company named Halifax plc. This important entity became a component of the best known London Stock Exchange index the FTSE 100. The company went through another name change in 2001 as it merged with the Bank of Scotland's The Governor and Company to form HBOS. The company's long and proud independent history ended in 2006 when an act called the HBOS Group Reorganization Act of 2006 transferred all bank assets and liabilities of the group over to the Bank of Scotland which also became a standard plc company holding Halifax as one of its divisions.

The new group ran into trouble in the financial crisis and had to be rescued. The HBOS began suffering from collapsing stock prices and rampant speculation on its future at the end of 2008. At this point, Lloyds Banking Group intervened and took over both Bank of Scotland plc and HBOS in January of 2009. Lloyds TSB applied to the Court of Sessions which approved them taking over HBOS in a January 12, 2009 ruling. Bank of Scotland along with HBOS officially became a part of the Lloyds Banking Group family on January 19, 2009.

Troubles continued after the merger. The Bank of Scotland announced on February 9, 2010 it would be closing its 44 retail bank branches in Ireland. The deteriorating economic environment and crisis were the reasons Halifax gave out for the closures. In August of that year, they announced that the last business of Bank of Scotland Ireland would be wound down by the conclusion of the year. This resulted from an over $2 billion loss they booked during the first six months of the year because of failed loans they made earlier to property developers.

International Bank for Reconstruction and Development (IBRD)

The International Bank for Reconstruction and Development proves to be a principal and original organization within the World Bank. It loans money to help out middle income nations as well as poorer countries that are creditworthy. It derives the majority of its funds from selling bonds on the global capital markets.

Over 180 countries participate as members of the IBRD. Every member has a certain amount of voting power. This is based on its subscription of capital. The United States possesses a full sixth of all the IBRD's shares. Besides an enormous amount of voting clout, the U.S. also owns the exclusive rights to veto any changes which are proposed for the bank itself.

The origins of the International Bank for Reconstruction and Development hail back to the end of the Second World War. The United States founded it in 1944. The initial purpose of this organization lay in assisting Europe to rebuild itself from the devastation brought on by World War II. The role of the bank has since shifted to offering loans along with technical assistance, knowledge, and advice to mostly middle income nations.

As the first institution within the World Bank, the IBRD cooperates closely alongside the other institutions within the World Bank Group. Together they serve to encourage economic growth, to assist developing nations in reducing the poverty of their citizens, and to help spread prosperity.

The bank itself is owned by the 189 member nations' governments. A board and directors represent these countries for routine decision making and administration. This board is comprised of 25 members who are Executive Directors. Five of these are appointed and 20 of them are elected by the owning members.

Developing nations are able to benefit greatly from the technical services, knowledge, and strategic advice that the bank provides. This is beyond its financial resources which it distributes as guarantees, loans, and risk management products. The World Bank serves in this capacity its beneficiaries who are also shareholders and global actors as well as being clients of the bank.

Not only national but sub national levels of governments can participate and benefit. The International Bank for Reconstruction and Development finances a wide variety of projects spanning every sector. It simultaneously offers its expert knowledge and technical support for varying phases in an ongoing project.

Some of the financial services and products which the IBRD delivers assist countries with developing resilience to external shocks. They help with product access for alleviating negative affects of interest rates, currency exchange rates, destructive weather and natural disasters, and volatility in commodity prices. The bank is different from a traditional commercial lender in that it does more than serve as a financier. It also has an important role in the international transfer of knowledge and technical assistance.

In times of crisis, the International Bank for Reconstruction and Development serves to help preserve the financial strength of its borrowers to limit the negative effects on the poor. It also works to provide financial market access to these nations at better terms than they would be able to attain by themselves. This helps with attracting private capital as well by encouraging a positive investment environment.

Many of the longer term social and personal development projects that the bank supports, private creditors would not consider. The bank also helps with promoting institutional reforms in areas like anti-corruption and public safety.

Jumbo Loan

Jumbo loans are specific types of loans made by banks for home mortgages. They are special because these loans are for larger sized house loans. In order for a loan to be qualified as a jumbo one, it must be larger than the conforming loan limits.

The government Federal Housing Finance Agency sets these conforming loan limits through regulation. They are the agency that oversees the mortgage buying government sponsored entities Freddie Mac and Fannie Mae. Both of these groups purchase mortgages from the traditional lenders like banks and credit unions.

For the majority of the United States, jumbo loan limits start at $417,000. There are several states and a few hundred counties that have different loan limit amounts. Some of these limits range as high as $625,000 for their loan limits in areas that are the most expensive property markets.

Counting Louisiana parishes, Alaska boroughs, and the District of Columbia like counties, the U.S. has 3,143 counties. This does not consider the Virgin Islands, Guam, or Puerto Rico. An overwhelming majority 2,916 of these counties have the traditional limit amount of $417,000 for jumbo loan minimums.

Another 115 counties have loan limits that are in between the typical $417,000 and $625,000 maximum. This would include higher than usual priced real estate markets but not the most expensive ones like Los Angeles. In Colorado Denver County is one such example with a jumbo loan minimum of $458,850. Another 108 counties contain higher jumbo loan limits that start at $625,500. Included in these are the most expensive housing markets. Among these are such pricey counties as those found in New York City, Los Angeles, and San Francisco.

Several states and their counties are allowed to have higher conforming loan limits than the maximum amounts set out by the government housing authority. This includes Hawaii, Alaska, the Virgin Islands, and Guam. These are all treated specially because of a long time exception to the regulation. In Hawaii for example, four of its five counties have the highest limits for jumbo loan cutoffs. They range from $657,800 to $721,050.

Obtaining a jumbo mortgage involves some extra paperwork and proofs. Underwriting for these jumbo types is much the same as with standard conforming mortgages. There are more requirements for appraisals and down payments than with smaller mortgages. Some jumbo mortgage lenders have a requirement for two appraisals rather than the standard single one.

Down payments are also often more demanding for jumbos than for the traditional mortgages. Usually these lenders will want a higher down payment to ensure the individual can really afford and is committed to the loan. The minimum down payments for these more expensive home purchases will vary with each lender. They might be as high as 30%, or they could be as low as 15% to 20%.

Only applicants with significant finances need apply for these jumbo loans. A great number of their lenders require a minimum high credit score of 700 or better. They also insist on a debt to income ratio that does not exceed 43%. These lenders will want to see minimally from six to twelve months' cash reserves in bank accounts as well.

Jumbo loans are not only made to individuals for their primary residences. Lenders will also issue them for vacation or second homes. Investment properties may also involve jumbo loans. They come with a wide range of terms and interest rates.

Jumbo loans can be issued as adjustable rate loans or fixed rate loans. They often come with higher interest rates than individuals would pay for conforming loans or for high balance conforming home loans. Sometimes in addition to the bigger down payment the underwriting standard will be stricter as well.

Laddering

Laddering is a strategy for managing overlapping CD maturities so as to not incur needless and potentially expensive early withdrawal penalties. Investors would employ such a strategy as this for a good reason. Consider that many savers will find that they covet the more substantial certificate of deposit rates offered on the longer term from three to five year (and even ten year) certificates. The problem is that they fear the uncertainty that comes with tying up their money for several years.

This is why investors would consider utilizing the effective certificate of deposit maturity management strategy of Laddering. The gist of this time tested and proven strategy revolves around investing in a range of different maturing CDs. Each single CD or group of CDs should have a variety of different lengths of terms. When each closest dated term certificate matures, the investors take the resulting proceeds and reinvest those in another CD that possesses the longest possible term.

The idea behind this is that some portion of the funds which the investor ties up in the certificates of deposit will nearly always be maturing. Should the investor require some portion of the funds then, he or she will be capable of accessing them without having to suffer early withdrawal penalties of from three to six months' worth of interest payments as punishment for breaking the time deposit.

With any complicated investment concept, it always helps to look at a real world example. This clarifies the idea by putting it in tangible terms that are easier to picture and grasp. Consider this following example. Perhaps an investor John has $100,000 to save and invest. John might divide the money up into five even lots. This would amount to $20,000 per lot. He could then take each $20,000 and invest it in a variety of maturing CDs. The best strategy in this case would be to put $20,000 in a one year CD, another $20,000 in a two year maturing CD, a third $20,000 into a three year CD, a fourth $20,000 into a four year CD, and the final $20,000 in a five year long certificate of deposit.

When the first year elapsed, John would have his shortest dated, one year maturity CD pay out. He would then take that $20,000 plus interest and place it into another five year term length time deposit CD. On the second year, he would similarly reinvest his take from the two year maturity time deposit into yet another five year long maturity certificate of deposit. Each year, he would continue to have one time deposit mature, and he would take those funds and ladder them into another five year deposit.

By repeating the Laddering procedure, within five years John will own five different five year long certificates of deposit (with one maturing every single year). This would provide him with the coveted flexibility he needs to cash in a time deposit CD each year and never risk the grueling penalties of early withdrawal should he need the funds.

It is important to realize that choosing to invest funds in time deposit CDs like this will never be the fastest means of increasing money, even when utilizing a Laddering strategy. It is similarly extremely safe and comes with very little risk. The government guarantee of principle for up to $250,000 per CD means that the money will be returned by either the bank, the FDIC Federal Deposit Insurance Corporation or the NCUA National Credit Union Administration.

By employing the laddering strategy, investors can at least capture those CD rates which prove to be the highest possible on the market. Should interest rates rise, then every year the investors are able to upgrade to a CD based on the higher then-current interest rates. This is a dependable way to make decent returns on savings money without having to tie it up for more than a year at a time.

Lender

Lenders are individuals or more commonly institutions that loan out money. The person who receives this money is a borrower. A number of different kinds of lending organizations exist. These include commercial, mutual organizations, educational, hard money, and lenders of last resort.

Commercial lenders are the most common of the traditional lenders. Commercial types are usually banks. Another kind of commercial lender would be a private financial organization. Commercial lenders provide offers on their loans to their borrowers at a set rate of loan terms. Such terms include time frame of the loan and the interest rate. Their goal is to make as much money as possible relative to the chances of the borrower not repaying the loan.

Mutual organizations are another type of lender. They are composed of members of the mutual who cooperate together to loan money to the membership. The members pool their money into the organization. From there it is loaned out to the members who need to borrow money. They do this with favorable terms and at advantageous rates.

Mutual organizations are not driven to make profits. This allows them to offer lower interest rates on the loans they make and higher interest rates on the deposits they take. Among these mutual groups are community based credit unions. Friendly Societies are another example of them.

Educational lenders provide loans to individuals who are looking to further their education at an institution of higher learning like a college or university. They offer borrowers subsidized or unsubsidized loans. When the loans are subsidized, the Federal Government guarantees the loans and ensures that the lender provides a low and often fixed interest rate.

Hard money lenders make special types of loans that are short term. These are loans principally secured by real estate collateral. The downside to this kind of a lender is that they often provide higher interest rates than a traditional commercial bank. The tradeoff is that they will often take on a larger variety of deals.

Typically these hard money lenders give terms that are more flexible to their borrowers. Some states have stricter laws on interest rates that may be charged than does the Federal government. This forces hard money lenders to operate under different rules and with lower interest rates when they are in conflict with usury laws in give states.

Many times these loans that lenders make to individuals become brokered loans. In such cases, third parties consider the borrower's case then send the loan request out to a variety of lenders. This is often done over the Internet. They pick these different lenders because of their chance of approving the borrower in question. Sometimes the terms can be improved by one or more of these competing lenders in order to win over the borrower's business.

Lenders of last resort are an interesting final category. They are often governmental organizations whose goal is to save national economies and important banks from failure. These types of organizations loan money out to too big to fail banks which are close to collapse. They do this to safeguard the bank's depositors and to prevent panic from pushing the nation's economy into a downward spiral.

Lenders of last resort can also be private organizations that make loans to individuals. These groups loan out money to borrowers who present great risks of default or who have extremely low credit scores. Interest rates with these lenders are substantially higher than with traditional lenders. They charge these rates in order to make up for the losses they suffer from their borrower's greater default rates. Such lenders that charge even higher rates are sometimes known as loan sharks.

Loan Servicing

The term loan servicing refers to the procedure of either a mortgage bank or servicing firm gathering up the regular principal and interest payments from the mortgage and loan borrowers. The amount of such service depends on the kind of loan in question and the particular terms that have been arranged between investors looking for such services and the servicing firm.

In the roaring days of the housing expansion, mortgage servicing got to be substantially more profitable than it had been in the past. Loan servicers sought out borrowers who were likely to have trouble making their payments on time. They did this with the hope of bringing in a greater number of lucrative late fees. After the financial collapse and in the Great Recession, this strategy came back to haunt them, as greater and greater numbers of homeowners defaulted on their mortgages and other types of loans.

Loan servicing outfits commonly make their money in the form of a percentage of the remaining balance on any loans that they are servicing. While the actual fees vary, they typically range from twenty five basis points down to a single basis point. This has much to do with the loan's size, amount of service necessary, and whether the loan is backed up by residential properties or commercial properties.

Loan servicers carry a certain value on their balance sheets from these loans. The current net value of the payment flow obtained in servicing the loans minus the anticipated costs for servicing them generates the asset that goes on the balance sheet. Such asset values commonly prove to be highly volatile when refinancing becomes more common. This is because the loans are commonly paid off in advance, leading to an end to the servicing fees that are collected.

A number of companies have traditionally been major players in the loan servicing field. These include Bank of America, JP Morgan Chase, Wells Fargo, and Citigroup as the biggest participants. GMAC is another major servicer. Between them they handle in excess of sixty percent of all American residential mortgage debt.

For special borrower cases that are near default or already behind, another industry of loan servicing has grown up. This is dominated by two companies. Ocwen Financial and Litton Loan Servicing, which Goldman Sachs owns, overshadow the industry. While it is the case that the big servicing companies are capable of handling borrowers who are unable or unwilling to pay, they do it inefficiently. As many as twenty-four different employees of the major loan servicing companies become involved from the first call of a collection agent down to the final foreclosure.

Loan Modification

A loan modification proves to be a set of changes on the original terms and conditions of a mortgage loan agreement. These must be agreed to by both the borrower and the lender. The housing crisis of 2007 caused many American homeowners to be on the verge of foreclosure. The numbers of imminent and in process foreclosures increased dramatically.

Loan modifications were amended to be a means for home owners to stay out of foreclosure and keep their houses. The process is not simple or quick, and it can be time consuming. Consumers also have to watch out for scams that prey on the vulnerable owners of homes.

Before the financial crisis erupted, a loan modification turned out to be a means for borrowers to ask for better interest rates on their mortgages without having to undergo an entire refinancing ordeal. Every mortgage company did not offer them. The ones that featured these would provide them for a cost to borrowers on the condition that their mortgage had not been resold to another firm. Now they are far more commonplace since lenders needed unorthodox solutions to help homeowners who were struggling to keep up with their payments and avoid foreclosure.

For the process of a loan modification to begin, the borrower must first request such a change to the loan terms. These changes once only affected the interest rate and made them lower. The more recent packages offered since the Great Recession are even able to change adjustable rate mortgages into standard fixed rate types. It is possible that a lender could suggest such a change to its borrowers as a possibility. Usually the borrowers initiate the process by determining they can not keep up with their loan payments and asking for help and a modification.

The next step is for the lender to consider the borrower's request. They are not required to agree to these petitions. A great number of lenders have very strict guidelines on which borrowers they will approve for modifications and which they will not. This is the case even when the homeowner has foreclosure looming. It is partly because such modification programs were not created to save home owners from rising adjustable interest rates or payments they could not handle. They were made to create a cheaper way of refinancing down to better interest rates. Each lender makes its own rules for which modifications they will accept and which they will reject.

Finally the lender will decide whether to approve or reject the modification request. They will then notify the borrower in writing. Many borrowers are rejected because they have been late with their mortgage payments frequently or too recently. Other lenders might not be in possession of the original loan any more. Whatever the reason is, the lender will state this in the letter.

If the request for modification gains approval, the request goes through to the department that handles loan servicing. There the loan will be modified to the new terms and conditions. Usually this will only reduce the interest rate and not change the loan's amortization. It may require several payment periods before these changes take effect. This is why borrowers should always keep making the payments in the amount and time for which they are scheduled.

London Interbank Offered Rate (LIBOR)

LIBOR is a main global benchmark interest rate. It stands for London InterBank Offered Rate. This rate represents how much banks actually charge each other for loans based on one year, six months, three months, one month, and overnight timeframes. Banks all over the world use this benchmark rate. Reuters news service publishes this critical rate every day at 11 am. They do this in five different currencies of the U.S. dollar, the Euro, British Pound, Swiss franc, and Japanese yen.

Historically the BBA British Bankers Association oversaw and compiled this rate. The IBA ICE Benchmark Administration assumed this responsibility on August 1st of 2014. They figure up this rate using contributor bank submissions. In every currency for which they calculate it there are between 11 and 18 contributing banks who act as an oversight board.

LIBOR does more than provide a rate for the interbank loans. It is utilized as a bank guide for their setting of credit card rates, interest only mortgages, and adjustable rate loans. Bank lenders add in between one and two points to make money. An incredible $10 trillion in loans are determined at least in part by this interbank rate.

Besides these uses, this rate also serves as a base price for credit default swaps and interest rate swaps. These contracts are a type of insurance in case loans default. The swaps also created the 2008 financial crisis. Hedge funds and banks believed that risk did not exist in the mortgage backed securities because they were protected by this insurance.

The problem arose as the subprime mortgages that underlay the mortgage backed securities started defaulting. AIG and other insurance companies discovered they did not have enough cash available to pay off the swaps. In order to save all swap holders from bankruptcy, the Federal Reserve was forced to rescue AIG with a bailout. Despite the fact that these swaps were supposed to be dispersed after the financial crisis, the LIBOR rate remains the basis on over $350 trillion of such credit default swaps.

Banks created LIBOR in the 1980s in response to a demand for a standard interest rate to establish derivatives. The original rate came out in 1986 in the three currencies the U.S. dollar, British pound, and Japanese yen. The

BBA later expanded it to include the additional currencies of Swiss franc and Euro.

A scandal plagued the LIBOR rate starting in 2012. The British Bankers' Association figured out the rate using its panel of banks that acted as representatives from every one of the currencies involved. BBA queried the banks about the rate they would charge in the set currencies for different amounts of time. The BBA's downfall was that they believed the rates the banks provided them with were true.

This unraveled in 2012 as British bank Barclays became charged with deliberately providing lower rates to the BBA then the ones they actually received from 2005 to 2009. They suffered a $450 million fine and the CEO Bob Diamond had to resign. When Diamond went down he told authorities the majority of other banks engaged in the same practice and that the Bank of England was aware.

The reasons that Barclays and others were lying about their rate was for better profits. Lower rates made the banks look stronger and more attractive to borrowers than banks with higher rates. The end result had three bankers found guilty of manipulating rates in 2015 while six others were acquitted of their charges in 2016. The guilty bankers all worked for Rabobank. The rate was taken away from the British Bankers Association and given over to the care of the ICE Benchmark Administration because of the scandal.

Mario Draghi

Mario Draghi has worn many hats in his career. He is currently the Italian economist, banker, and manager who took over the role of European Central Bank President from his predecessor Jean-Claude Trichet on November 1, 2011. Before this, he has been professor, director at the World Bank, head of the Italian treasury, and board member at a number of companies including Goldman Sachs. Forbes has listed Draghi as the eighth most powerful individual on earth in 2014. Fortune magazine named him the second greatest leader in the world in 2015.

As professor, Mario Draghi worked in the political science department of the University of Florence beginning in 1981 through 1994. He also served in the capacity of fellow at the Institute of Politics at Harvard University in 2001. While professor at Florence, the Italian held the job of Italian Executive Director for the World Bank during the years 1984 to 1990. The next year, he took on the post as Italian Treasury general director, a post he held a decade until 2001. In this capacity, he chaired the important committee that reworked Italian financial and corporate legislation and wrote the laws which govern the financial markets in Italy.

During the years from 2002 to 2005, Mario Draghi worked at Goldman Sachs as their managing director and as vice chairman for the Goldman Sachs International group. In his time there, he worked with important governments and corporations throughout Europe implementing the company's development and strategy in the continent. This caused controversy when he was later being considered for the post of European Central Bank President.

Goldman had been involved with the credit default swaps that helped Greece to disguise its true financial situation before the global financial crisis broke out in 2008 and 2009. His defense centered on having not known anything about the arrangements and having nothing to do with it. All the deals Goldman Sachs had arranged with the government of Greece had been finalized before he joined Goldman.

Mario Draghi took on the job of Bank of Italy Governor in December of 2005. He served in this role until October of 2011. During this time, he was a Board of Directors member at the Bank for International Settlements. He also was European Central Bank Governing and General Councils member during this tenure. He remains Italy's governor on the board for the Asian Development Bank and the International Bank for Reconstruction and Development.

The greatest challenges for Mario Draghi have been since he was elevated to succeed Trichet as the President of the European Central Bank on November 1, 2011. He will serve in this capacity through October 31, 2019.

Mario Draghi has overseen the three year $640 billion loan program that the ECB ran for the European banks from the end of 2011. Under his leadership, he repealed his predecessor's two rate hikes. He also increased government bond purchases of nations which were struggling in the periphery of the euro zone to help combat the debt crisis.

In July 2012 when the sovereign bond crisis renewed, he announced the ECB would do whatever was necessary to preserve the Euro. Since that statement, the bond yields and borrowing costs have declined especially for Italy, Spain, and France. His verbal intervention has been called one of the critical turning points in the euro zone's fortunes.

Mario Draghi continues to fight economic stagnation in the euro zone. The bank mostly does this with its negative interest rates policy. They also continue aggressive quantitative easing every month as stimulus programs to support weak growth throughout the continent. In these and many other actions throughout his career, Draghi has demonstrated he deserves his nickname "Super Mario." He originally received this name for his incredible ability to survive Italian politics.

Maturity

In the world of business and finance, maturity stands for the last payment date of either a loan or some other form of financial instrument. It is also known as the maturity date. On this maturity date, both the outstanding principal and any remaining associated interest are owed and expected to be rendered for final payment. If they are not paid on the maturity date, such loans or instruments are considered to be in default.

A fixed maturity pertains to a kind of financial instrument where the loan will have to be paid back on a pre set date. Included in fixed maturity instruments are variable rate loans and fixed interest rate loans or other kinds of debt instruments. Besides these, redeemable preferred shares of company stocks fall under this category of fixed maturity instruments. The key to fixed maturities is that they must have a particular maturity date spelled out in their terms. This maturity date is much like a redemption date.

Other instruments do not come with a set fixed maturity date. These kinds of loans go on indefinitely, until the point that a lender and borrower get together and agree on the loan being paid down. These instruments and loans are sometimes referred to as perpetual stocks. Other financial instruments may include a range of potential dates of maturity. These types of stocks may be repaid at any time that suits the borrower, so long as it is within the time range that is provided to them.

Another form of maturity is the serial maturity. Serial maturities mostly pertain to bonds that companies issue to borrow money for a variety of purposes, including expansion into new markets or developing and marketing new products. With serial maturities, all of the bonds are actually issued at one time. Their classes describe the various redemption dates on them, which are generally staggered away from each other.

Maturity is also used by financial news media to discuss securities that have maturities, such as bonds themselves. This abbreviation for these kinds of investments is commonplace. They might claim that the yields declined on twenty year maturities. This would mean that bond prices which are due to reach full maturity in twenty years rose while their actual yields fell, since bond prices move inversely to the direction of their associated yields.

All types of bonds may be referred to using this short hand form of calling them maturities. This could include corporate bonds, Federal Treasury bonds, and also local government municipal bonds. All of these bonds have specific dates of maturity on which they will repay their principal. Preferred stocks also could be thought of as maturities, since they similarly possess set dates on which they are redeemed. They are not commonly referred to by this abbreviation though.

Monetarism

Monetarism is an idea that Milton Freedman developed and expounded upon. It centers on the idea found in monetary economics that money supply changes lead to huge impacts on short term national outputs and on long term price levels. It argues that the goals of monetary policy are most effectively achieved when the money supply is carefully and appropriately expanded in line with actually output growth.

Milton Friedman started out as a believer in Keynesian economics. Later in his career, he determined that it had major problems and he began to criticize it on a variety of levels. He wrote a book with Anna Schwartz that proved to be extremely influential. In this book, "A Monetary History of the United States 1867-1960," Friedman proposed that inflation is everywhere and always a monetary phenomenon. Because of this now generally accepted truth, he strongly recommended a policy to be practiced by the central banks, or the Federal Reserve, of maintaining supply and demand equilibrium of money. This money supply should only increase with demand and accompanying productivity growth.

The roots of monetarism come from two radically opposed concepts. The hard money policies of the end of the nineteenth century were merged with some of the monetary ideas held by John Maynard Keynes who argued for money supply that was driven by demand. Keynes concentrated on the stable value of a currency that had been threatened by a lack of sufficient money supply that then led to currency collapse. Friedman concentrated instead on price stability to control and keep down inflation. This proves to be the perfect equilibrium of demand and supply for money. Friedman took these diametrically opposed concepts and wove them together into a new theory of Monetarism.

In the 1960's and 1970's, this Monetarist school of thought for monetary demand being a stable function found significant traction in the work of David Laidler. Other influential monetarists include former U.S. Federal Reserve Chairman Alan Greenspan, who showed his Monetarism bias in his own policies and ideas. Some central banks have attempted to orient their monetary policy around appropriate targets for money supply. The European Central Bank is the chief of these Monetarist idea central banks.

Monetarism is not entirely without its critics. The neo Keynesians propose that money demand and supply are closely interrelated. Other conservative economists maintain that monetary demand is not predictable. Nationally known economist Joseph Stiglitz makes the case that the relationships that exist between the growth of the money supply and inflation are weak at times when inflation is actually low.

Money of Zero Maturity (MZM)

Money of zero maturity represents a way of measuring the money supply. This measurement for money which is circulating in an economy only covers money that is available to be spent and utilized. As such, this MZM is really a counting of all of the money supply that is liquid in a given economy.

Individuals can figure up the money of zero maturity with some basic math. This starts with obtaining the M2 measure of the money supply. From this M2 figure, all time deposits must be subtracted, such as with certificates of deposit. Next this result must be taken and added to the amount of money market funds which are available. This sum finally provides the MZM.

In practical terms, this measure of money includes several different components. All physical currency, including bank notes and coins, are a part of it. Checking account balances are also included. Savings account totals similarly comprise the MZM. Finally, money market accounts round out the figure. These are all configurations of money which are immediately available for par value to both companies and individuals.

Other forms of money are not included in the measure. Money of zero maturity never considers money held in accounts such as certificates of deposit or any other types of time deposits. This is because these funds contained in such financial instruments can not be instantly accessed for full par value. Similarly investments held in stocks and bonds must be first sold and settled before they can be obtained.

A number of analysts like to utilize the money of zero maturity because it proves to be an extremely liquid measurement. In fact this has grown to become among the most preferred means of measuring the country's money supply exactly because it does more completely depict the readily available money in the economy that can be employed for consumption and other spending. The name for this money measure comes from its combination of all available liquid and money with zero maturity that the three M's contain in M1, M2, and M3.

There are practical applications for the money of zero maturity measurement. The figure presents a reliable indicator of a nation's actual money base for the entire economy. As such it depicts the quantity of money which is literally moving throughout the economy as a whole. Since the Federal Reserve quit tracking and following the M3 number for money supply back in 2006 on March 23rd, this has become a preferred measurement of money supply, if not the most popular one.

When economists and analysts are aware of the amount of money which is moving throughout the economy, they can develop a feeling for two important trends. They are able to learn at a fairly quick glance whether or not the economy is growing or is instead contracting. By studying this figure, they can also determine how high the danger for inflation is over the near term.

When economists look at a chart of the MZM, they are interested in the rate of growth on a year to year, quarter to quarter, or month to month basis. As this growth rate improves, the economy is likely to expand along with it, and the threat of inflation increases apace. If instead the growth rate in the MZM decreases, the economy stands a solid chance of shrinking. This would mean inflationary threats are lower.

Money Supply

Where business and economics are concerned, the money supply proves to be the complete quantity of money that is available throughout the economy at any given moment in time. Money can be defined in a few different ways. The commonly accepted definitions are comprised of both circulating currency and demand deposits. Demand deposits are the assets of depositors in banks that are easy for them to access, such as checking accounts.

The statistical data on money supply is recorded and made available to the public by the government. In some countries, the central bank publishes such information. Analysts are always interested in any changes to the money supply total, since it has great impacts on inflation levels, prices, and the business cycle.

There are now several different measurements of money supply published within the U.S. These range from narrow to broad money supply totals. While narrower calculations only measure the most liquid of assets that are easy to spend, such as currency itself and checking account deposits, other broader measures include assets that are not so liquid, such as certificates of deposit.

The MB is the complete monetary base as it pertains to all currency. It proves to be the money supply figure that is the most liquid. M1 is the measure that leaves out bank reserves. M2 is the measurement that is given as the main economic indicator in figuring how high inflation will become. Both money and its near substitutes are included in this category. M3 used to be the main figure for money supply in the Untied States, until the Fed elected not to release it any longer after 2006. It included the M2 measure plus longer term deposits.

Inflation commonly results from changes to the money supply. The evidence demonstrates the direct correlation between the growth of the money supply and longer term rising prices. This is particularly the case when the money supply increase is rapid within an economy.

The latest example of how the growth of the money supply can ruin a currency and destroy an economy is demonstrated by Zimbabwe. This

African country witnessed dramatic increases in the national money supply and then became a victim of hyperinflation, or a dramatic gain in prices. Because of this, the money supply has to be responsibly controlled and overseen.

The money supply is actually controlled through monetary policy. Central banks such as the Fed determine the money supply in part through their reserve ratios that they make banks observe with percent of deposits kept on hand. They can also adjust it with the interest rates that they set for the country.

Many critics have pointed to the rapid growth in the money supply of U.S. dollars in the years of the financial crisis and the Great Recession as dangerous. From the years of 2007-2010, the dollar money supply has been grown by in excess of three hundred percent. At the same time, the economy has a whole has barely grown. This is the consummate recipe for inflation, and many economists have suggested that you will see high inflation, and potentially even hyperinflation, within the United States in the next several years as a direct result.

Morgan Stanley

Morgan Stanley is one of the two major American investment banks (along with Goldman Sachs) that survived the financial crisis of 2008/2009. It is an international financial services company that has headquarters in New York City in the Morgan Stanley Building. The firm has over 1,300 offices and employs around 60,000 staff. The group has operations in 24 countries. The company boasted $1.454 trillion in assets under management for 2014. This impressive figure represented a gain of 17.5% over the 2013 numbers.

The investment bank originally arose on September 16, 1935 as a venture of the partners of J.P. Morgan & Co, Henry S. Morgan (grandson of legendary J.P. Morgan) and Harold Stanley. The company was forced to split off its investment banking business from the commercial bank operation because of the Glass Steagall Act. This first year of the new investment bank saw it gain a 24% market share of both private placements and public offerings, amounting to $1.1 billion at the time.

These days Morgan Stanley offers financial institutions, governments, and individuals investment products and services. Today the firm has three principal areas of business. These are Institutional Securities, Global Wealth Management, and Investment Management.

In recent years, the Institutional Securities division has proven to be the biggest profit maker for the company. This component offers services like raising capital and financial advising services to institutions. This includes help with restructuring, advising mergers and acquisitions, corporate lending, and project and real estate financing.

Global Wealth Management delivers the company's investment advising and brokerage services and products. The present division came about when the group's wealth management merged with Smith Barney. Citigroup originally held a 49% stake in this joint venture until Morgan Stanley bought out its stake entirely. The segment offers high net worth clients wealth planning and financial services.

The group's Investment Management division offers products and services for asset management across a variety of asset classes. These include fixed income, equity, real estate, alternative investments, and private equity. Both retail and institutional clients are able to participate in these offerings that the group delivers through their institutional distribution network, intermediaries, and third party retail distribution networks.

During the financial crisis, the firm swung bank and forth between hero and victim in the saga that rocked traditional banks and investment banks to their core. The U.S. Treasury originally contracted them to provide advice on a possible means of rescuing Freddie Mac and Fannie Mae in August of 2008.

Yet the company itself proved to be in trouble as its market value plunged more than 80% between 2007 and 2008. As its stock price continued to slide and the company suffered heavy losses on home building related companies, it began to consider merger possibilities with a variety of other banks. Among these were HSBC, Standard Chartered, Wachovia, Citigroup, Nomura, and Banco Santander. When the investment bank fell into serious trouble during the height of the financial crisis, Treasury Secretary Hank Paulson offered to hand Morgan Stanley over to JPMorgan Chase for free. CEO Jamie Dimon turned down the offer.

On September 22, 2008, Morgan Stanley and Goldman Sachs the last of the big American investment banks declared they would change into traditional bank holding firms which the Federal Reserve would regulate. The Fed approving this bid to become traditional banks brought an end to the power of the securities firms 75 years after the events that segregated them from traditional lenders. It also ended a number of weeks of market chaos that had caused Lehman Brothers to file for bankruptcy and Bank of America to rush purchase Merrill Lynch & Co.

Ultimately Morgan was saved both by a $107.3 billion loan from the Federal Reserve, which represented the largest loan taken by any bank, along with a $9 billion investment by largest Japanese bank Mitsubishi UFC Financial Group.

Mortgage

Mortgages are loans made on commercial or residential properties. They commonly use the house or the property itself as collateral. These mortgages are paid off in monthly installments over the course of a pre determined amount of time. Mortgages commonly come in fifteen, twenty, and thirty year periods, though both longer ones and shorter ones are available.

A variety of differing mortgages exist. All of them have their own terms and conditions that translate into advantages and disadvantages. Among the various mortgage types are fixed rate mortgages, adjustable rate mortgages, and balloon payment mortgages.

The most common kinds or mortgages, especially for first time home buyers, prove to be fixed rate mortgages. This is the case because they are both simple to understand and extremely stable. With such a mortgage, the regular monthly payments will be the same during the entire life of the loan. This makes them very predictable and manageable. Fixed rate mortgages have the advantages of protection against inflation, since the interest rate is locked in and can not go up with the floating interest rates. They allow for longer term planning. They come with very low risk, since you are always aware of both the payment and interest rate.

Adjustable rate mortgages, also known as ARM's, have become more popular since they begin with lower, more manageable interest rates that result in a lower initial monthly payment. The downside to them is that the interest rate can and likely will go up and down in the loan's life time. Factors to consider with ARM's are the adjustment periods, the indexes and margins, and the caps ceilings, and floors. The adjustment period is the one in which the interest rate is allowed to reset, commonly starting anywhere from six months to ten years after the mortgage begins.

The interest rates change based on the index and margin. The interest rates are actually based on an index that is published, whether it is the London Interbank Offered Rate, or LIBOR, or the U.S. Constant Maturity Treasury, or CMT. The margin is added to this index to determine the total new interest rate on your mortgage. The amount that these ARM rates are capable of going up or down in a single adjustment period and for the life of the loan is called a cap, a ceiling or a floor.

The third common type of mortgages is balloon reset mortgages. They come with thirty year schedules for repayment, with a caveat. Unless you pay are willing to allow the mortgage to reset to then current interest rates at the end of either a five year or seven year term, then your entire balance will be due at this point. This gives you the benefits of the low monthly payment plan as a person with a thirty year loan would have, yet you will have to be willing to pay off the whole mortgage if you do not take the reset option when the term is up. Because of this, many people refer to this type of a mortgage as a two step mortgage.

Mortgage Costs

Mortgage costs are fees that real estate transactions incur when it is time for them to close. The point for closing comes as the seller transfers the title to the property over to the buyer. Mortgage costs can be absorbed by the seller or the buyer. A number of different expenses go into these overall costs.

The amount for mortgage costs ranges dramatically based on the property the individuals are buying and where they live. They cover many different expenses. There are fees for such things as credit reports, attorney costs, and appraisals. A survey fee pays for the expense of confirming where the property lines are. Pest inspection fees pay to check for termites and other home damaging insects.

Credit report fees pay for running the borrower's credit. Inspections may be requested by the lender or the buyer, and there is a fee for these. With the loan origination fee, lenders receive their compensation for handling all of the loan paperwork on behalf of the borrower. They receive a separate amount called an underwriting fee when they evaluate the application for the mortgage loan.

Other mortgage costs have to do with discounts, titles, and escrows. Discount points turn out to be optional fees that borrowers pay to receive a more favorable interest rate on the loan. A title search fee pays to have a background check performed on the title to ensure that there are no problems like tax liens or unpaid mortgages attached to the property.

Lenders also insist on title insurance. This insurance protects them against a title that turns out not to be clear. The recording fee goes to the county or city to compensate them for adding the update to the land records. There could also be an escrow deposit. This provides for several months of the private mortgage insurance and property tax costs.

Even though mortgage costs vary wildly from one region to another, it is still possible to estimate how high they will be. Home buyers can anticipate commonly paying somewhere between two percent and five percent of the final price of the house in closing fees. This means that if a house costs $200,000, the mortgage costs could run from $4,000 to $10,000.

The law requires that lenders provide home buyers with a Loan Estimate that covers the amount that these fees will approximately be. They must do this in three days or less of accepting the loan application. These are estimates that will change on a number of the fees.

Three business days or more before the closing occurs, the lender will provide borrowers with a Closing Disclosure statement. This covers the actual closing fees. It is a good idea to hold this up to the original Loan Estimate to contrast the expenses. The lender should explain every item on the fees, why they are important, and why they differed from the original estimate.

In many cases, a significant number of these costs can be negotiated. Some of them can even be removed as unnecessary. This includes fees such as courier, mailing, and administrative costs that the lender is attempting to collect. Borrowers always have the option of walking away from this particular loan if the fees seem high and unreasonable. Other lenders will be agreeable to provide competitive loans with more reasonable fees.

There are also no closing cost mortgages. In these, borrowers are able to sidestep the fees upfront when they close on the loan. Lenders still make money by exacting a higher interest rate or by rolling the costs into the whole mortgage. This last method causes borrowers to pay interest for the mortgage costs as well. Sellers can occasionally be persuaded to absorb the fees at closing.

Negotiable Instruments

Negotiable instruments are documents which agree to provide payment to a particular individual known as the assignee. The individual who receives this payment is called the payee. This party usually has to be named or somehow mentioned on the instrument itself. One type of negotiable instrument is a check. Checks are negotiable instruments that can be transferred. These signed documents promise that they will pay the check bearer the specified amount on demand or on a future specified date.

There are other types of negotiable instruments that individuals and businesses use. Some of these are promissory notes, bills of exchange, certificates of deposit, and drafts. These negotiation instruments can be transferred which is part of what makes them so popular. The holder is allowed to receive the funds in cash or to utilize them in a different manner as they see fit.

The dollar amount specified on these documents comes with notes regarding the exact amount that has been promised by the payer. The funds have to be rescinded in full as specified or on demand. Negotiable instruments are allowed to be transferred from one individual to the next. After the instrument is fully transferred, the bearer gains complete legal title to the instrument and its promised funds.

Such documents can not be set with additional conditions or instructions regarding payment beyond the date and sum to be paid by order of the instrument. They do not deliver any additional promise from the group or person issuing the negotiable instrument besides the promise to pay that specific amount.

After nearly 150 years of existence, the check still remains the most typical form of negotiable instruments. This draft is payable by the financial institution of the payer once received and for the precise amount that is clearly mentioned. There are various other kinds of checks too. Cashier's checks also do the same task. They require that the funds be set aside or allocated for the person who will receive them before the check itself can be issued. They are guaranteed funds in essence and not simply a promise to pay someone an amount. Money orders are much like checks.

The main difference is that they might or might not be issued by the financial institution of the payer. As with cashier's checks, the money has to be paid in from the payer to the issuer in advance of the money order being printed up and finally issued. After the money order is in the hands of the payee, it can be changed in for cash according to the terms, policies, and conditions of the issuer in question.

Traveler's checks are yet another form of negotiable instruments. They have a tighter security mechanism than the other forms of instruments. Their system requires two full signatures in order for the transaction to be completed. These types of checks can also be replaced if they are lost or stolen. When the traveler's checks are first issued, the payer has to sign on the document itself to offer a signature sample.

After the payer decides to whom he or she will issue the payment, the individual must offer a countersignature in order for the payment to be made. These negotiable instruments are most often utilized when the payer is traveling abroad and needs a more secure form of payment which delivers a higher security feature in case they are stolen or defrauded while out of the country.

Offshore Banking

Offshore Banking is a means of banking by keeping your funds in a bank that is outside of the country in which you primarily reside, or literally "offshore." These days it has acquired a negative connotation consistent with money laundering, criminal activities, or tax evasion. Yet none of these mental pictures are accurate any longer. All an offshore bank account truly means is that it is overseas or international. When individuals choose to keep part of their bank deposits internationally, this is a sensible, legitimate, and legal practice.

The old model of the Swiss Offshore Banking account has expanded to numerous other countries. Today places as far flung as Singapore, Hong Kong, Panama, Malta, Liechtenstein, Bermuda, Jersey, the Isle of Man, Gibraltar, and the Cayman Islands all participate in the concept. Some of the highest-rated and most financially stable Offshore Banking centers are Singapore, Hong Kong, and Liechtenstein.

There are a number of good reasons why ordinary people (as well as wealthy clients) opt to move their checking and savings accounts overseas to an Offshore Banking center. For starters, this protects assets from legal or government malfeasance. It is not an exaggeration to claim that any individuals who choose to maintain all of their assets and funds within the exact same country in which they work and live are taking on substantial legal (and hence financial) risk. The United States proves to be by far the most litigious society and nation which has ever arisen in all of world history. It is the shocking truth that any government agency or court can freeze any individual's private bank accounts with only one phone call and with no due process.

A second good reason for using Offshore Banking concerns the fact that the banks in other countries outside of most Western nations are far safer and sounder financially. Many banks in the so-called first world or developed world are in perilous financial condition. This became painfully obvious back in 2008 during the Western-based Financial Crisis and Great Recession. Some of the largest American, British, and European banks failed or went to the brink of bankruptcy. Examples of this are Wachovia Bank, Washington Mutual Bank, Bear Stearns, Lehman Brothers, and Merrill Lynch.

Many others would have gone under but for desperate and generous government support of the likes of Citibank, Royal Bank of Scotland, and Lloyds TSB. While many of them have recovered somewhat, others like Credit Suisse, UniCredito, and Deutsche Bank remain in dangerous financial condition. In fact in Europe there are even entire banking systems as in Italy, Greece, Spain, Ireland, and Cyprus that had to receive sometimes multiple bailouts in order to survive at all. The jury is still out on the large and too big to fail Italian banking system.

American banks also keep dangerously low levels in their liquidity. This means that they do not have nearly enough cash and cash equivalent assets to pay their depositors back in the event of a customer "run on the bank." Yet in Offshore Banking centers like Malta, Singapore, Hong Kong, and Liechtenstein, the banks are conservative to a fault. They practice extreme caution with their depositing customers' money and keep huge and conservative liquidity and capital ratios. Many of these same jurisdictions are governments with little to no debt and highly solvent and very well-capitalized banking insurance funds.

Finally, Offshore Banking centers often pay significantly higher interest rates for U.S. dollar deposits. While major Western central banks in the United States, Great Britain, Europe, and Japan have absolutely slashed their interest rates to historic low rates or even negative interest rates, others are still paying decent returns overseas. In some of these, investors can receive even in excess of four percent on U.S. dollar-denominated deposits in low to no risk banks and regulatory regimes and jurisdictions.

Peer to Peer Lending (P2P)

Peer to Peer Lending helps consumers who have some extra money to invest to help out those who need to borrow it. It is often abbreviated as P2P Lending. The idea behind peer to peer lending is not a new one. It has grown exponentially online in the past ten years thanks to the Internet. The benefits of this form of lending are that it reduces usurious interest rates dramatically. This means that both consumers and the overall economy benefit as it decreases the amounts of payday loans.

Prosper is one of the largest P2P lending companies in America. It loans out amounts as high as $35,000. For this they charge a closing fee of 5%. Their interest rates range from 5.9% for extremely good credit to 30% for credit that is only fair. These rates are often lower than what credit card companies charge and substantially lower than payday loan companies which can command over 600% in a single year.

Loans with Peer to Peer Lending companies like Prosper are unsecured. The applicants' credit history earns the approval, though it does not require perfect credit to obtain them. The money itself comes from surplus money which normal people across America wish to invest.

These Peer to Peer Lending companies generally allow their loans to be utilized for most any type of need. They encourage ones that are financially responsible. Debt consolidation is one of the big reasons why individuals take out these loans. The interest rate is often more affordable than the ones the credit card companies charge. Such a loan helps individuals to pay off loans quicker and with a larger amount of the money attacking the principal rather than interest.

Home improvement is another commonplace reason that consumers employ these peer to peer loans. The traditional means of financing such loans comes from bank issued home equity loans or lines of credit as well as from credit cards. The home equity loans often require a great amount of time for approval and commonly include expensive fees. This has encouraged smart home renovators to seek out Peer to Peer Lending companies.

Small businesses like these loans which help them to increase their capital for expansion. Traditional banks will often require a lot of paper work and documentation in order to issue an approval. P2P lending operations such as Prosper only need credit scores that are decent.

Many consumers have turned to these companies for financing for car loans as well. Having this money pre-approved and in hand can save more than just dealer approved financing costs. It can strengthen the buyer's hand in negotiating the final price on the vehicle as the money for the purchase is effectively offered to the dealer in cash instead of financing.

One of the many advantages to these Peer to Peer Lending companies is that they do not charge early repayment penalties. This makes them effective financing vehicles for many different types of needs. Individuals have employed them in place of short term loans and to pay for surgeries not covered by insurance, among other uses.

Besides this, P2P lenders do not require the prime credit scores that most banks do. Consumers can access substantial loans of as much as $35,000 with credit scores that start at a fair 640.

Plunge Protection Team (PPT)

The Plunge Protection Team is a nickname given to the President's Working Group on Financial Markets. It came into existence to make economic and financial recommendations on the economy when there are periods of economic chaos. On the team are the heads of the most critical U.S. financial regulatory organizations. This includes the Secretary of the U.S. Treasury, the SEC Securities Exchange Commission Chairman, the Chairman of the Federal Reserve, and the Chairman of the CFTC Commodity Futures Trading Commission.

The Washington Post newspaper created the nick name Plunge Protection Team only a decade later in 1997. President Ronald Reagan originally convened the team as a response to the terrible Black Monday stock market crash. The government was desperate to restore investor confidence in U.S. financial markets. President Reagan called together the group to improve on the efficiency, integrity, and order of them.

The Working Group on Financial Markets was instructed to find out what happened with the financial markets in the U.S. on and around trading day October 19, 1987. They were told to come up with government actions for coordinating efforts and making contingencies to prevent them from happening again when possible.

To carry this out they were told to talk with various representatives from the business world. This included individuals from clearing houses, exchanges, significant market players, and regulating bodies to learn what the market might suggest for non-government solutions.

Finger pointing at first characterized the investigation. The NYSE held the various futures exchanges responsible for the crash. The CME group engaged in a number of studies to refute this by having market experts rationally analyze the events. They refuted the accusations for the problems with these studies.

One positive mechanism came from these initial meetings with the Plunge Protection Team. NYSE and CME group worked to establish circuit breakers between the securities and futures markets. This slowed down or stopped wildly erratic moves in the market. These circuit breakers remain in effect to this day.

The PPT had 60 days from the Executive Order to give this initial report to the President. They were to report from time to time after this as they reached more findings and solutions for recommended changes to the legislation. When the report and finished recommendations were completed, the President did not disband the group as many had expected.

Instead it stayed together to be reconvened on any subsequent crisis and threat to the financial system. This caused some observers to believe that the group had a secret purpose to manipulate markets and ensure they stayed higher. The group covered such issues as the almost collapse of Long Term Capital Management, Terrorism Risk Insurance from September of 2006 and Over the Counter Derivatives Markets and the Commodity Exchange Act in November of 1999.

Most famously the group reconvened during the financial crash of the Great Recession in 2008. In March, 2008 they issued their Policy Statement on Financial Market Developments. It had the PPTs analysis and report on what continued to plague the markets and cause the ongoing market turmoil.

Their final conclusions had to do with the subprime market mortgages. The determined that the main cause of the destructive chain of events started with the rise in delinquencies of these mortgages. They issued another statement on the continuing crisis on October 6 of 2008. In this they announced that the situation in worldwide financial markets continued to be very strained. They assured investors that they were working with global regulators and market participants to take on the problems and restore stability and confidence to markets.

Private Mortgage Insurance (PMI)

PMI is the acronym for Private Mortgage Insurance, also known sometimes as Lenders Mortgage Insurance. PMI proves to be insurance that is paid to a lending institution that is required much of the time when an individual gets a mortgage loan. Such insurance is used to cover any losses that arise if a person is not capable of paying back their mortgage loan.

Should the lender not be able to recoup all of its costs in foreclosing on and selling the mortgaged property, then PMI insurance covers the remaining losses that exist on the balance sheet of the bank or other lender. The general rates for this Private Mortgage Insurance turn out to be around $55 each month for every $100,000 that is actually financed. On a $250,000 loan, this amounts to $1,875 each year in premiums.

Private Mortgage insurance yearly costs range though. They are usually given out in comparison against the entire loan's value. This depends on a number of factors, such as loan type, loan term, actual coverage amount, amount of home value that the person finances, the premium payment frequency that might be monthly or yearly, and the individual's credit score. While PMI can be paid in advance with closing costs, it can also be worked into the loan payments with single premium PMI.

Private Mortgage Insurance is generally only necessary when the down payment proves to be smaller than twenty percent of either the appraised value of the property or alternatively of the sales price. When then loan to value ratio is greater than eighty percent, you can expect to be required to carry it. As the principal is reduced with monthly payments, or the home value rises through real estate appreciation, or a combination of the two occurs, then this Private Mortgage Insurance might not be required any longer. At this point, the home owner is allowed to discontinue paying for the PMI insurance.

There are some banks and lenders who will insist that PMI be paid for minimally for a pre fixed period of time, such as two to three years. This is regardless of whether the principal value of the property exceeds eighty percent in a shorter amount of time. Banks do not have to permit a person to cancel this insurance legally until the loan has amortized down to a Loan to Value ratio of seventy-eight percent of the original price for which the house is purchased.

A cancellation request must originate from the mortgage servicer. They must send it to the issuing company that made the PMI policy in the first place. Many times, such a mortgage servicer will insist on a current home value appraisal being done in order to ascertain the actual loan to value ratio.

Premiums paid for mortgage insurance were not tax deductible according to the Internal Revenue Service in the past. In 2007 this changed. Now all PMI premiums are considered to be fully reducing of your income for the year in question.

Quantitative Easing

Quantitative easing is the policy where the government purchases bonds and financial instruments by printing money in order to stimulate the economy. Quantitative easing proves to be a monetary policy that the Federal Reserve and other central banks around the world utilize in order to grow the money supply. They do this by boosting the cash reserves in the banking system. This is accomplished via purchasing the government's issued bonds in order to raise their prices.

Since prices and interest rates of bonds move inversely, higher bond prices lead directly to lower long term interest rates. Quantitative easing is commonly employed only after other more traditional means of dominating the supply of money have not worked. These other methods involve lowering discount rates, bank interest rates, and even interbank interest rates to around zero.

Once these traditional means have failed to stimulate the economy, the Fed then steps into the market and directly buys financial instruments. The assets that they purchase include agency debt, government bonds, corporate bonds, and mortgage backed securities, which they purchase from banks and institutions. This entire process is called open market operations. By depositing electronically created money into the banks' accounts, the banks gain additional reserves that permit them to create still additional money from thin air. The Fed hopes that this multiplication of deposits accomplished through the fractional reserve banking system will allow greater amounts of loans to be made to businesses and individuals in order to stimulate the economy.

This quantitative easing policy is not without its risks. It could be too effective or not sufficiently effective, should banks decide to hoard their extra money to boost their capital reserves. This is particularly the case in an environment of rising defaults in the banks' mortgage and other types of loans' holdings.

Recent examples of quantitative easing abound. This subtle form of printing money became more and more common as the financial crisis of 2007 to 2010 grew worse. In these years, the United States engaged heavily in it, tripling the world wide dollar reserves by creating money both at home and abroad. Other Central Banks, such as those of Great Britain and the European Union, similarly engaged in the practice to help mitigate the effects of the crisis and resulting Great Recession. These countries and economic blocks had all already lowered their interest rates to zero or near zero amounts, and they found quantitative easing to be their best remaining option for restarting economic growth.

Refinance

When the word refinance is used, it is referring to the act of refinancing, or canceling out a currently existing debt with another debt that a bank or refinance company issues under alternative terms. By far and away the most popular refinancing that pertains to consumers is for mortgages on houses. Debt replacements that are performed in conditions of financial distress are also known as debt restructuring.

Home owners might choose to refinance their mortgage for a variety of reasons. It can assist them in meeting a range of end goals. You as a home owner might be interested in lowering your monthly payments on the mortgage through attaining a better interest rate or lengthening the terms of the loan.

You could lessen the amount of interest that you pay during the loan's term and expand the equity build up by going through a refinance to get a loan with a shorter life. You could also decrease your exposure to the risk of rising interest rates through obtaining a fixed term loan in place of a balloon mortgage or adjustable rate mortgage. Finally, you might be interested in drawing out home equity in order to do debt consolidation or to cover the costs of major expenses that you are encountering elsewhere.

The act of refinancing eliminates the original mortgage loan. This is then replaced with a new loan. There are many factors that you will have to decide in obtaining this new loan. This includes what type of loan is most ideal for the circumstances, which lender you will utilize, which term and rate are most advantageous, and the fees that you feel are reasonable. Because of these complicated decisions that must be made, consumers should seek out advice in their refinancing. If you do not possess a clear comprehension of all that is involved with the refinancing procedure, then you could accidentally put your house or your finances in danger.

There are risks associated with refinancing. These are principally penalty clauses that are also known as call provisions. When you pay off a mortgage loan early, these penalties would be triggered along with closing fees. The refinancing itself will entail transaction fees. All of these fees should be figured up and considered before you begin a project to refinance your home loan. This is especially the case since all of the fees together may eliminate any potential savings that you hoped to realize through the refinancing.

Another possible downside to refinancing loans is that they may provide you with lower payments every month on the same amount of money to be repaid. In this case, you will pay a greater amount of interest throughout the loan term. You would also pay on the debt for a great number of additional years over the original mortgage's terms. This is why it is so important to determine not only the upfront charges, but also the variable and ongoing costs involved in refinancing as a factor in the decision on whether to pursue it or not.

SDR Denominated Bonds

SDR denominated bonds are a fairly recent phenomenon. These are bonds issued in special drawing rights currency units. SDR units are a basket of the world's most important currencies including the U.S. dollar, Euro zone euro, Japanese Yen, British pound sterling, and the Chinese Yuan. The International Monetary Fund's executive board approved a framework to issue such bonds to member nations and central banks back on July 1, 2009.

The principle of these SDR denominated bonds was intended to be allocated in SDRs. The market for such bonds was established initially as the official sector of IMF members. This meant it was to include primarily the member nations, relevant central banks, and another 15 holders of SDRs.

Included in these 15 prescribed holders are four central banks which were regional, eight developmental organizations, and three monetary agencies which were intergovernmental. Others allowed to trade in them were the fiscal agencies of the members. This means that a number of sovereign wealth funds were allowed to participate as there are not always distinguishing lines between national monetary authorities and their sovereign wealth funds. This is the case with Hong Kong and Saudi Arabia.

The IMF issued SDR denominated bonds were to start with three month maturities that could be extended to as long as five years. Interest payments on these instruments were quarterly. China signed an agreement to buy upwards of $50 billion of them, while Russia, India, and Brazil intended to buy as much as $10 billion each.

SDR denominated bonds again gained the international spotlight in August of 2016 when the World Bank's IBRD International Bank for Reconstruction and Development priced the first such bond in the Interbank Bond Market of China. This bond raised 500 million SDR units, which were equal to about $700 million US dollars. These bonds came with a three year maturity date. Their coupon interest payment rate was .49% per year. What made them most notable was that the payments are issued in Chinese Yuan.

This group of bonds is only the first batch. The full size of the issue approved by the World Bank SDR Denominated Issuance Program in August 12, 2016 is for 2 billion SDR's, making them equal to roughly $2.8 billion US dollars.

Even in China, placing so many SDR denominated bonds is a challenge. This is why the joint lead managers for the Interbank Market were several important banks with great depth in China. These included HSBC Bank of China Company Limited, the Commercial Bank of China Limited, China Development Bank Corporation, and China Construction Bank Corporation.

The issue was a great success. The significant interest in them led to a 2.5 times oversubscribing. Orders amounted to roughly 50. Fifty-three percent of them came from bank treasuries, 29 percent from central banks and official institutions, 12 percent from asset managers and securities firms, and six percent from insurance companies. These bonds will mature on September 2, 2019 with all payments coming from the World Bank's IBDR to be made to bond holders in Chinese Yuan.

Societe Generale

Societe Generale is a French banking giant that proves to be among the largest financial services companies in Europe. As of 2015, it boasted 31 million customers living in 66 countries where they have branches. A staff of 146,000 employees works for the bank and comes from 122 different nations. The bank counts 31 million customers that include private individuals, companies, and financial institutions.

The French Societe Generale subscribes to the universal bank model that attempts to offer all types of financial services to its clientele. They base their model on a combination of businesses that serve France and people around the globe. The bank relies on its expertise in its core businesses. These include retail banking, corporate and investment banking, financial services, private banking, insurance, and asset management. Combining all of these businesses, they are able to provide a full complement of financial products and services for the many different needs of their customers.

The French retail banking group operates under three different brands. Societe Generale is their nationally leading bank. Credit du Nord is comprised of a number of different regional banks. Boursorama represents the largest online bank in France. These different bank brands provide for the financial needs of 11 million different individuals and around 810,000 corporate, professional and not for profit customers. This group has a goal to be the leading French bank for safety and customer satisfaction.

Societe Generale also operates a major international retail bank as well as a consumer credit operation. This services more than 32 million customers living in 52 countries. This business adapts the universal bank concept to the needs of the local market.

The group's Societe Generale Corporate and Investment Banking is responsible for the investor and institutional client needs. They act as a go between for investors and issuing groups in four key activities. These are financing, investment banking, investor services, and market activities.

Financial services provides offerings under three core businesses. These are the Insurance, Vendor and Equipment Finance, and Vehicle Leasing and Fleet Management businesses. They help the group to develop powerful synergies in the dozens of countries where the bank has a presence.

The bank turns out to be among the biggest and most important private banks in the world. Their Private Banking division provides high net worth individuals with various strategies. These include portfolio management, markets and funds wealth management, and asset allocation solutions.

Insurance is an activity the bank carries out through two agencies it owns in France. Sogecap is their life insurance company. It tailors a wide range of insurance offerings for corporate, professional, and individual clients. These include life insurance, personal protection, and retirement savings plans.

Sogessur is their accident insurance and property insurance provider. This company delivers insurance packages for people in categories life insurance, personal accident, car and home insurance, school insurance, and others. The company insurance line operates as a leading provider in 13 different countries. For life insurance it holds a rank as number six in France, number two in the Czech Republic, number four in Morocco, number five in Luxembourg, and number seven in both Russia and Romania.

Asset management includes a range of different securities services and offerings under the Societe Generale Securities Services division. Among these are custody and trustee services, clearing services, liquidity management, retail custody services, asset servicing and fund administration, global issuer services and fund distribution.

They also have a subsidiary group Lyxor Asset Management. This company provides advising and asset management services for all types of asset classes. Lyxor is a leader for transparent, flexible, and creative asset management.

Swiss Interbank Clearing (SIC)

Swiss Interbank Clearing is the interbank clearing system that Switzerland uses for payments within the country and between its banks. SIX Interbank Clearing Limited launched the system on June 10, 1987. They have been operating it since then for the Swiss National Bank.

The primary eligible users of the SIC are all of the Swiss banks along with German Post Finance. Cash handling companies, insurance companies, and securities dealers which are based in either Switzerland or Liechtenstein are also able to participate. The system allows for foreign based banks to utilize it once they fulfill the added requirements and conditions which the Swiss National Bank sets.

Swiss Interbank Clearing handles large transactions as well as retail transfers that connect service providers to the banks. This includes automatic debits, card payments, and bank transfers. The system has grown continuously in the amount volume it settles and quantities of transactions it processes since SIX first launched it.

Ten years after SIX created and launched the Swiss Interbank Clearing, they developed a similar system to enable the Swiss financial center and Liechtenstein to have access to the European Union's TARGET2 clearing system. This is called the euro Swiss Interbank Clearing, or simply euroSIC. It permits Swiss banks settle any payments in Euros between themselves quickly, simply, and cheaply. Thanks to this expansion of the system, they do not have to keep mutual euro accounts. It saves them the additional trouble, paperwork, and expense.

EuroSIC also makes it possible for Swiss and Liechtenstein banks to send payments in real time to other Euro zone banks. The participating members can process Euro payments across borders with almost any Euro zone institution. The system works effectively both ways. Euro zone banks and institutions gain convenient access to more than 3,200 banks and branches throughout both Switzerland and Liechtenstein.

Banks and financial institutions which the Swiss National Bank supervises may participate in euroSIC. This also applies to any of their branches, joint institutions, or clearing organizations that are located outside the country of

Switzerland. These groups must be able to demonstrate that they have a comparable amount of operational and legal standards in the countries where they are based as do their partners or parent organizations in Switzerland.

The Swiss Euro Clearing Bank manages the system. This joint venture between SIX, UBS, Credit Suisse, and Post Finance bears the responsibility for both monitoring and supervising the euroSIC system. SECB has the advantage of being a German licensed bank as well. This means it provides a link to the real time clearing system of the Deutsche Bundesbank.

The system manager the SECB Swiss Euro Clearing Bank provides access to make rapid payments to Germany. The payments which euroSIC processes must be non urgent payments. Banks can send as much as much as 50,000 euros on behalf of their clients with reasonable transaction costs thanks to the system that the Deutsche Bundesbank provides. This is handled through the German EMZ bulk payment system. The SECB also provides its euroSIC members with a means for making inexpensive transfers and payments using the STEP2 system. This is the European Union wide bulk payments system.

Euro Swiss Interbank Clearing operates using the settlement accounts of the member institutions. SIX actually runs the system in Zurich, the Swiss financial center. Every transaction processes through the settlement accounts. There must be enough funds in the bank's account in the system at the Swiss Euro Clearing Bank for the transaction to go through in real time. Otherwise, the transaction is put aside until enough funds are present to cover the transaction.

Trustee Savings Bank (TSB)

Trustee Savings Bank refers to a now defunct type of British financial institution. It is also known by its acronym TSB. These banks began as savings deposit institutions for those who had only meager financial means. The shares of these banks were not stock market exchange traded. Rather they were something like the mutually owned building societies of Great Britain. A key difference between the two types of financial institutions was that the depositors of the TSB's did not have any voting rights or ability to direct the organization's managerial or financial goals and direction.

In consequence for a lack of owner-voting rights, the boards of directors for the Trustee Savings Banks were appointed as volunteer basis trustees. This explains where the name for the TSB's came from in the first place. Reverend Henry Duncan from Ruthwell in Dumfriesshire established Britain's very first TSB in Scotland. He set this up to help out his poorest members of the congregation in 1810. The only reason for the organization lay in serving the local community members.

During the inter-war years a hundred years later, the Trustee Savings Bank model demonstrated that it could effectively compete throughout the retail banking model market with the major commercial banks and building societies throughout the nation. At one point by 1919, these types of financial institutions counted an impressive 100 million British pounds in combined deposits and assets. This amount reached 162 million pounds by 1929 and an incredible 292 million pounds at the outbreak of the Second World War in 1939.

Despite enjoying two centuries of success and growth as independent institutions, the Trustee Savings Banks became combined into one financial institution called the TSB Group plc from the years 1970 to 1985. Their stock traded on the famed London Stock Exchange until 1995 when the group merged with the Lloyds Bank to become the enormous conglomeration Lloyds TSB. At that moment, the new Lloyds TSB combined unit represented the largest bank in the United Kingdom by market share. It was second only to HSBC by market capitalization, as HSBC has absorbed Midland Bank in 1992.

The group which now represented the legacy of the Trustee Savings Banks expanded again in 2009 with the acquisition of the HBOS Halifax Bank of Scotland group. Its name changed again to the Lloyds Banking Group at this point. The TSB name was not lost, as the primary retail banking subsidiaries were Lloyds TSB Bank and Lloyds TSB Scotland. Lloyds again resurrected the TSB name and brand when it divested the 632 branches from Scotland, Gloucester, Cheltenham, and some of the Welsh and English Lloyds TSB bank branches into the TSB Bank plc.

The new operation came into being on September of 2013 and underwent an IPO initial public offering during 2014. The rest of the Lloyds Banking Group changed its name back to Lloyds Bank. This spin off happened because the Lloyd's Banking Group had to be bank rescued by Her Majesty's Government. Thanks to the 43.4% government stake in the group as a result of the Global Financial Crisis, European Union state aid rules required that it spin off a portion of the business.

Trustee Savings Bank plc did not continue for long as an independent entity. It began life in 2013 with a national network of 631 bank branches throughout especially Scotland, and also England and Wales. They counted over 4.6 million customers as well as more than 20 billion British pounds worth of customer deposits and loans. The group had its headquarters in Edinburgh, Scotland.

As the reestablished TSB, the group had a listing on the London Stock Exchange and remained a member of the FTSE 250 index of British based companies until it received and accepted a takeover bid from Spanish-based bank Sabadell. Sabadell made its offer for TSB Bank in March of 2015 and completed the acquisition of the last remaining Trustee Savings Bank on July 8, 2015. TSB Bank still operates as a wholly owned subsidiary of Sabadell, so the TSB brand name remains.

UBS

UBS is one of the major Swiss and international banking giants. The group is a global firm that has its headquarters in both Zurich and Basel. The bank offers a variety of financial services to corporate, private, and institutional customers. The bank recently celebrated its 150 year anniversary in 2012.

The UBS Group has a presence in every major financial center of the world. They maintain offices in more than fifty different nations. The bank employs around 60,000 individuals in these global locations. Around a third of the bank staff work in the Americas. Switzerland is home to 35% of its employees. Eighteen percent of them work in the Europe, Middle East, and Africa region, while 13% of the group's staff are located in Asia Pacific.

In 150 years time, UBS has merged with and acquired in excess of 300 different banks. The long history of the bank helps to explain why it has evolved into a gold standard in the international banking sector and remains a cornerstone of the legendary tradition of Swiss banking.

In Switzerland today, the country operates approximately 300 branches and maintains 4,500 employees. They serve one out of three households and reach 80% of all Swiss wealth. The bank also provides accounts and services to 120,000 companies and 80% of the banks that call Switzerland their home market.

The bank prides itself on the financial products and services it delivers to its corporate, wealthy, and institutional clients around the globe and to Switzerland. Besides its Corporate Center, the bank operates in five principle divisions. These are Wealth Management, Wealth Management Americas, Asset Management, Personal and Corporate Banking, and the Investment Bank. They focus all of their endeavors in the business areas in which they excel. Because of this, they have significant and competitive positions in each of their markets.

The UBS Wealth Management business offers advice to the bank's global wealthy clients besides those in its Americas' group. The group offers its clients many solutions. These include investment management, wealth planning, lending and banking services, advice for corporate finance, and special offerings.

Among the foremost wealth managers in the Americas is the group's Wealth Management Americas. They measure this based on the invested assets and productivity of their financial advisors. The sub-divisions include Canadian Wealth Management and U.S. Wealth Management businesses along with any international business that books within the United States. This business serves high net worth and ultra high net worth clients.

The UBS Asset Management operates in 22 different nations. It provides a range of investment styles and capabilities in both traditional and alternative classes of assets. These provide these offerings to global wealth management customers, wholesale intermediaries, and institutions. This group is the biggest mutual fund manager in Switzerland, a foremost European fund house, Asia's biggest international asset manager, and among the biggest managers of real estate on earth.

The UBS Personal and Corporate Banking business delivers a wide host of financial services and products to the institutional, corporate, and private customers who reside in Switzerland. It is a leader in this market. This business is key to their universal bank model in the country. It refers its clients to the Wealth Management business after it helps them to reach a certain level of assets.

The group's investment bank delivers services to its institutional, corporate, and wealth management customers. It offers them creative solutions, expert and professional advice, competitive execution, and all inclusive access to the world's global capital markets.

In 2015, the group boasted revenues of 30.6 billion Swiss francs and operating profit of 5.5 billion Swiss francs.

UniCredit

UniCredit turns out to be the largest Italian based bank and one of the biggest banks in the continent. This banking group is a major player throughout Western, Central, and Eastern Europe. As a leading commercial European bank, it operates in 17 different nations and maintains over 143,000 employees. The bank counts on its retail network of more than 7,500 branches as well as an international network that covers 50 different markets. This group's commanding position in Western, Eastern, and Central Europe helps them to have what is among the highest market shares in the region.

UniCredit is also unique in its commitment to keeping the local brands of the banks that they combined with when they formed their banking group. This is evident in such names for its banks in other countries as UniCredit Bulbank. Here the group merged the Bulgarian market leader Bulbank brand with its own name. They believe that their local brands are extremely valuable and worth preserving when they acquire them.

The banking group is headquarter registered in Rome while its general management offices are in the Italian commercial center of Milan. UniCredit's principle markets are Italy, Bulgaria, Austria, southern Germany, Russia, and Poland. They have divisions for investment banking internationally in such markets as London, New York, Hong Kong, Munich, Milan, Budapest, Vienna, and Warsaw.

This banking group concept is a fairly recent construct. It originated from the merger of a number of Italian banks back in 1998. The biggest of these were Unicredito from Verona, Turin, and Treviso and Credito Italiano that included Banca Popolare di Rieti and Rolo Banca. The new group initially went by the name Unicredito Italiano before this was changed to its present form. From 1998 to 2000, the group acquired four other significant Italian banks. In 1999, the bank created a new subsidiary named for the original component Credito Italiano.

This international bank is run as several different divisions. These include the CIB, CEE, and national divisions for Italy, Germany, Austria, and Poland. CIB has the responsibility of Global Division for the group. It handles multinational clients and large corporate clients. These have the potential needs for products in investment banking. CIB also carries the responsibility for the Financial and Institutional Groups clients, for the Global Transaction Banking, for the International Activities, and for the Global Financing and Advisory businesses.

The CEE division helps to coordinate the various activities of UniCredit in the markets of Central and Eastern Europe. Its main goal is to bring them into a unified and comprehensive vision for the region. Under this division, the various national businesses besides Germany, Austria, and Poland operate. This includes the bank subsidiaries in the Czech Republic, Slovakia, Romania, Bulgaria, Serbia, Slovenia, Croatia, and Russia.

The Italian division handles many different business located in Italy under its leadership responsibilities. These client segments include First, Business First, Family, Corporate Banking, Private Banking, Asset Gathering, and Public Sector. The Italian division breaks down into seven geographical regions, a Real Estate Network, and a Private Bank Network.

Each of the main national divisions has its own head that reports directly to the Deputy General Manager. These include the core markets of Austria, Germany, Poland, and the CEE. The banking group is a complicated organizational structure that somehow works together to form one of the largest banks in Europe and internationally.

Wells Fargo

Wells Fargo has been one of the big four U.S. banks since its acquisition of Wachovia in 2008. This ranks it with JPMorgan Chase, Citigroup, and Bank of America. The bank grew to be the third biggest U.S. bank counted by assets as of the conclusion of 2015.

Ranked by home mortgage servicing, deposits, and debit cards, it is the second biggest American bank. Globally it figures as high as second largest bank in the world by market capitalization. The mostly U.S. focused bank is so large that in 2015, Forbes Magazine Global 2000 ranked it as the seventh biggest public company in the globe.

At the end of 2015, Wells Fargo Bank counted 8,700 retail branches with 13,000 ATM machines, over 100,000 employees, and 70 million customers. Though it is primarily a U.S. centered financial institution, it does maintain operations through 35 countries. These international centers mostly cater to large business corporations and other banks, and are not consumer or small business operations.

The present day shape of Wells Fargo Bank resulted from a merger and acquisition. In 1998, the Wells Fargo & Company merged with Norwest Corporation of Minneapolis. The bank's Financial Crisis era 2008 acquisition of Wachovia, based in Charlotte, North Carolina, allowed the company to become one of the dominant U.S. based financial institutions. It transferred the headquarters of the absorbed banks to its historic headquarters city of San Francisco where its original bank has been based since 1852.

The bank originally arose as a single subsidiary of the Wells, Fargo & Co. that Henry Wells and William Fargo founded in San Francisco to serve the West of the United States. Their new company in 1852 began offering both banking services via buying gold and selling bank drafts guaranteed by gold and express services. The express division offered quick delivery of gold and any other items of value around the West and eventually the entire country.

The present day company's corporate symbol hails from its days of operating the overland stagecoach line in the 1860s, of which the Pony

Express became a part. This service provided mail and business delivery via the fastest transportation available, including stagecoach, railroad, steamship, telegraph, and pony rides.

By 1888 the company's stage lines connected the country as the United States' first nationwide express operation. This service peaked at 10,000 locations throughout the U.S. before the Federal Government assumed control of the national express network as part of the World War I endeavors. The seizure left the company with only its single Wells Fargo & Co's Bank in San Francisco that had separated from the Wells Fargo & Co Express in 1905.

The bank spent the rest of the 20th century rebuilding and expanding. It went from a banker's bank in 1923 serving the whole West to a California statewide consumer bank in the 1980s. At this point it was the seventh biggest bank in the United States until the merger and acquisition catapulted it into the big four American banks.

Today Wells Fargo Bank offers its U.S. customers a wide range of products and services including checking and savings accounts, mortgages, credit cards, student loans, financial planning, insurance, business banking, and business and personal loans. Outside of the U.S. it does not have branches which provide consumer or small business customer services.

It does offer large businesses, corporations, and other banks services in 35 countries which include foreign banking, foreign exchange hedging strategies, exporting and importing, global supply chain finance, international payments, currency risk management, and help expanding into foreign markets.

Zombie Banks

Zombie banks prove to be financial institutions that in reality have literal economic net worths of less than zero. They still keep running because they are able to continue paying their debts using government's real or implied support for their credit and balance sheet. Although this term has come to be heavily used in the financial crises of 2007 to 2010, it did not originate there.

Instead, Edward Kane coined the phrase Zombie Banks back in 1987. He used it to refer to and relate the perils of allowing a great number of banks that were actually insolvent to continue operating. The phrase came to be utilized for the Japanese banking crisis that began in 1993. It once again arose in popularity during the financial crisis of the last few years where hundreds of banks have failed in single years.

Zombie banks have many problems. Among these are bank runs from frightened depositors who are uninsured for their full account values. They also suffer from margin calls from their counter parties in derivatives contracts.

Zombie banks can be deceptive, as on the surface they may look like they are actually healthy and have the necessary level of capital to run. As investors learn the fair value of their assets, then they are suddenly looked at as insolvent institutions. This is to say that Zombie Banks keep operating in a regular manner as if nothing is wrong with their balance sheets. Yet the truth is that they will likely be seized by the Feds when the word becomes wide spread that they do not have the assets and money that everyone believed.

Healthy banks are able to make loans to new borrowers at the same time that they honor their obligations to lenders and share holders. Insolvent banks, or Zombie Banks, are incapable of generating new loans, since they lack the money and capital to make such loans while still performing on their obligations to lenders and share holders.

Comprehending what constitutes a Zombie bank requires that you know the basics of a bank balance sheet. One side of a balance sheet actually contains a bank's assets. The other side is comprised of the bank's liabilities as well as the bank's equity. The two sides are supposed to equal out, which is expressed in the equation assets equal liabilities plus the bank equity.

Zombie banks manage to hide their problems since no one is able to determine how much their assets are really worth. Asset backed securities and collateralized debt obligations are examples of assets whose values can not clearly be determined at any given moment. They might be worth as much as seventy-five cents for every dollar, or they could be valued as low as twenty-five cents per dollar.

The problem comes when Zombie banks have over valued their assets. If they later are forced to revalue them to correct and more appropriate levels, they quickly discover that they no longer have the assets to cover their future liabilities. Admitting to this causes them to become Zombie banks. At this point, the bank share holders are typically wiped out, while the depositors are given their money back by the Federal Deposit Insurance Corporation.

American Bankers Association (ABA)

The American Bankers Association, or ABA, is a trade association of the U.S. banks large and small conveniently located in Washington, D.C. This powerful lobbying organization hails back to 1875 when it was established by several bankers.

Today, the ABA has grown to represent banks of all stripes and sizes and encompasses more than 95% of all bank assets in the nation. This means that money center banks, regional banks, community thrift banks, mutual savings banks, savings and loans associations, trust companies, and large commercial banks all count the ABA as their voice before the federal government. The typical sized member bank boasts around $250 million in assets.

This trade and industry group proves to be the biggest banking trade association by far within the U.S. today. It is also known as the biggest financial trade group anywhere in the United States. The American Bankers Association thrives and prospers because of its impressive range of both services and products it delivers to member institutions. This includes help in such diverse industry segments as insurance, staff training and education, asset management, capital management, consulting, and risk-compliance endeavors.

Probably the most famous creation of the American Bankers Association remains the all important nine digit routing numbers which designate all banks everywhere within the U.S. These routing numbers are pictured on every single check and are also necessary identification for wire transfer transactions. The ABA can truthfully boast that it created this system over a hundred years ago, way back in 1910.

Today's American Bankers Association keeps extremely busy lobbying with Congress for its banking members and their common interests. The group has concentrated its efforts in the last several years on banning the so-called unfair tax exempt status enjoyed by credit unions. Credit unions originally catered to selective and tiny targeted memberships, as with a particular company's own employees. This did not threaten commercial banks and other similar financial institutions.

More recently though, to bank's undying enmity and impotency in the face of this real and rising threat, credit unions found the means to vastly expand their roles of membership and possible pools of customers. It is no exaggeration to state that numerous credit unions can boast over $1 billion in assets nowadays. This makes them as big as some of the larger and even too big to fail banks.

The ABA strenuously maintains that such credit unions have morphed into a structure and operations which are so similar to the traditional commercial banks that they no longer deserve this special favor of tax exempt status. It was actually the infamous Panic of 1873 that gave rise to the initial founding of the American Bankers Association. A banker James Howenstein of St. Louis, Missouri, one day discovered that he was up against a proverbial wall in his bank. He only possessed several hundred dollars in cash against his millions of deposits he needed to return back to panicking depositors.

By falling back on assistance and knowledge willingly provided by his peers in the banking business via rapid and frequent correspondence, Mr. Howenstein escaped from his business-threatening dilemma to survive. He then knew that he had been saved by this informal network and fraternal organization of fellow bankers and wanted to expand on this successful construct.

To this effect, Mr. Hownestein convened his first meeting of 17 different bankers on May 24, 1875 in New York City. Together they made plans for an initial American Bankers Association convention that did successfully take place on July 20, 1875 in Saratoga Springs, New York. Fully 349 different bankers who hailed from 31 states as well as the nation's capital attended.

Chief among the first endeavors of the ABA proved to be setting up the American Institute of Banking. They founded this in 1903 in order to offer certificates and examinations as professional banking education in their local branch chapters. This AIB offered interested participants a different way to pursue a banking career than by going to university for a degree in law and finance.

Annual Percentage Rate (APR)

The annual percentage rate, or APR, is the actual interest rate that a loan charges each year. This single percentage number is truthfully used to represent the literal annual expense of using money over the life span of a given loan. Annual percentage rate not only covers interest charged, but can also be comprised of extra costs or fees that are attached to a given loan transaction.

Credit cards and loans commonly offer differing explanations for transaction fees, the structure of their interest rates, and any late fees that are assessed. The annual percentage rate provides an easy to understand formula for expressing to borrowers the real and actual percentage number of fees and interest so that they can measure these up against the rates that other possible lenders will charge them.

Annual percentage rate can include many different elements besides interest. With a nominal APR, it simply involves the rate of a given payment period multiplied out to the exact numbers of payment periods existing in a year. The effective APR is often referred to as the mathematically true rate of interest for a given year. Effective APR's are commonly the fees charged plus the rate of compound interest.

On a home mortgage, effective annual percentage rates could factor in Private Mortgage Insurance, discount points, and even processing costs. Some hidden fees do not make their ways into an effective APR number. Because of this, you should always read the fine print surrounding an APR and the costs associated with a mortgage or loan. As an example of how an effective APR can be deceptive with mortgages, the one time fees that are charged in the front of a mortgage are commonly assumed to be divided over a loan's long repayment period. If you only utilize the loan for a short time frame, then the APR number will be thrown off by this. An effective APR on a mortgage might look lower than it actually is when the loan will be paid off significantly earlier than the term of the loan.

The government created the concept of annual percentage rate to stop loan companies and credit cards issuers from deceiving consumers with fancy expressions of interest charges and fees. The law requires that all loan issuers and credit card companies have to demonstrate this annual percentage rate to all customers. This is so the consumers will obtain a fair comprehension of the true rates that are associated with their particular transactions. While credit card companies are in fact permitted to promote their monthly basis of interest rates, they still have to clearly show the actual annual percentage rate to their customers in advance of a contract or agreement being signed by the consumer.

Annual percentage rate is sometimes confused with annual percentage yield. This can be vastly different from the APR. Annual percentage yield includes calculations of compounded interest in its numbers.

Annual Percentage Yield (APY)

APY describes the amount of compound interest which individuals or businesses will earn in a given year (or longer time period). Investments in money market accounts, savings accounts, and CD Certificates of Deposit all pay out such interest. It is the annual percentage yield that demonstrates precisely the amount in interest individuals will receive. This is helpful for people or businesses trying to ascertain which investments and banks offer superior returns by comparing and contrasting their real yields. In general, higher Annual Percentage Yields are better to have (unless one is comparing interest on credit card debts).

This APY is practical to understand and measure simply because it considers compound interest and the miracle of compounding within any account. Simple interest rates do not do this. Compounding is simply earning interest on interest that has already accrued and been paid. It signifies that individuals are gaining a greater amount in interest than the corresponding interest rate literally indicates.

It is always a good idea to consider a real world example for clarification purposes. If Fred deposits $10,000 into a particular savings account that provides a two percent yearly interest rate, then at the end of that first year Fred will have $10,200. This assumes that the interest is paid one time per year. If the bank were to figure up and pay out the interest on a daily basis, it would increase the amount to $10,202. The extra $2 may seem small, but given a longer time frame of from 10 to 30 years, this amount can add up, particularly if larger deposits are involved.

APY should never be confused with APR. They have some similarities, but APR does not consider compounding. It is once again a simpler means of computing interest. Credit card loans are an area where it is important to understand the differences between annual percentage rate and annual percentage yield. When people carry a balance, they will be paying higher APY's then the APR the firm actually quotes. This is because interest is assessed monthly, which means that interest on the interest will be computed on each following month.

The key to obtaining a better APY on investments and savings accounts lies in getting as frequent a compounding period as possible. Quarterly compounding is better than annually, yet daily is the most superior form of compounding possible. This means that as individuals are looking to increase their APY's personally, it is important to have the money compounding as frequently as they can practically achieve.

When two CD Certificates of Deposit pay out the same rate, it is best to select that one which actually pays out both more frequently and also boasts the greater APY. With CD's, the interest payments become automatically reinvested. More frequent reinvestment is always better. This will help any individual or business to earn a greater amount of interest on the interest payments already earned and paid out.

Calculating the annual percentage yield is not an easy task. Business calculators as well as computer algorithms mostly do it for people nowadays. The simplest way to find the APY for a given account is to plug in the information including the initial deposit, compounding frequency period, interest rate, and amount of overall time for the period considered. These smart calculators will then tell you both the effective annual percentage yield as well as the ending balance on the hypothetical account at the end of the given time period.

Assumable Loan

An assumable loan is one that permits a home buyer to take over, or assume, a home seller's contract on their mortgage. This is not permitted by every mortgage lender in the place of a typical home purchase. Loans that do not have Due On Sale clauses, such as the majority of VA and FHA types of mortgages, can usually be assumed and are considered to be assumable loans.

Assumable home loans work in the following manner. A current home owner will simply transfer over his or her mortgage contract and obligations to a purchaser who is qualified to take over. In the past decades of the 1970's and 1980's, these types of mortgage note assumptions proved to be quite popular. Back then, they could be done without even having to obtain the mortgage lender's authorization. These days, the only types of mortgages that may be assumable loans without needing a lender's actual permission are those that are made by the FHA or VA.

Assumable loans provide opportunities for both buyers and sellers. It is often the case that a home buyer will not be able to secure a better rate for a new mortgage than that provided by an already existing mortgage. This could result from the negative credit history of the buyer in question or the conditions existing in the market place at the time. As existing interest rates rise, the appeal of non-existent lower rates on mortgages commonly pushes prospective home buyers to look out for assumable loans. Such a home buyer who secures an assumable loan then has the responsibility for the mortgage that the home seller previously carried.

The existing rates of the mortgage carry over for the buyer as if the person had made the original contract themselves. This assumable loan process also saves the buyer a number of the settlement costs that are incurred in making a new mortgage. This can be a substantial cost savings benefit.

Sellers similarly benefit from assumable loans. It is not uncommon for sellers to wish to be involved in the savings that buyers realize in the process of transferring over an assumable loan. Because of this, the two parties commonly share in the savings.

As an example, when the sale price of the home in question is greater than the amount owed on the mortgage itself, then the buyer will often have to put down a significant down payment, which goes straight to the home seller in this case. Otherwise, the buyer might have to get another mortgage to come up with the difference in amounts. A seller's principal benefit in participating in such an assumable loan transfer lies in having a good chance of getting a better price for the home.

Alan Greenspan

Among the various Chairmen of the Board of Governors for the Federal Reserve System over the years, Alan Greenspan stands out as a living legend. He began his nearly two decade term as Federal Reserve Chairman on August 11, 1987 and then served all the way through January 31, 2006. An unprecedented four different sitting presidents appointed Alan Greenspan as chairman of the Fed. During his time in the most important economic office in American, Greenspan made such ideas as "irrational exuberance" household phrases.

Alan Greenspan began his famed career working for the non profit outfit the National Industrial Conference Board. Here he analyzed the demand for aluminum, steel, and copper. During the years of 1954 to 1974 and 1977 to 1987, Greenspan served as president and chairman of Townsend-Greenspan & Company at the New York City based economic consulting firm.

President Gerald Ford brought Alan Greenspan into government service where he served from 1974 to 1977 as the President's Council of Economic Advisers chairman. President Ronald Regan utilized his services in several capacities, first as the National Commission on Social Security Reform chairman from 1981 to 1983. Later he worked on the Economic Policy Advisory Board for President Reagan, as well as consultant to the CBO Congressional Budget Office.

Once Alan Greenspan took over as Board of Governors chairman for the Fed, he faced a crisis just months after assuming the post. This came in the form of the stock market crash Black Monday of October 1987. He moved rapidly to make certain liquidity continued to exist in the various markets. While head of the Federal Reserve, Greenspan led the nation through two recessions, the 1997 Asian Financial Crisis, and the 9/11/2001 terrorist attacks.

During this lengthy tenure in office, Greenspan gained a reputation as being staunchly against inflation and concentrating his efforts and firepower on maintaining stable prices more than on delivering full employment. Numerous economists and historians give Greenspan great credit for overseeing and assisting the lengthiest economic expansion in American history. He earned a deserved reputation for his ability to build up consensus among his various colleagues at the Fed Open Market Committee where policy was concerned.

Alan Greenspan has served in numerous roles in both the public and private realms. He worked for several presidents on appointments that included the Commission on Financial Structure and Regulation, the President's Foreign Intelligence Advisory Board, the Commission on All Volunteer Armed Force, and also the Task Force on Economic Growth. Besides this, Greenspan has worked as a corporate director at a number of corporations. These include The Pittston Company, Mobil Corporation, Morgan Guaranty Trust Company of New York, J.P. Morgan & Co., General Foods, Capital Cities/ABC, Automatic Data Processing, and Alcoa the Aluminum Company of America.

After Alan Greenspan resigned from the Federal Reserve Board of Governors, he started up his own Greenspan Associates, LLC consulting firm in Washington D.C. He also published his official memoirs on his time in office in 2007 as The Age of Turbulence.

Greenspan is remembered for several of his famous quotes on irrational exuberance, money printing, and the gold standard. Regarding the ability of the United States to pay its mounting debts to its many creditors, he claimed, "The United States can pay any debt it has because we can always print money to do that. So there is zero probability of default." This reinforced the truth of a quote he had made decades earlier regarding inflation and the gold standard. "In the absence of the gold standard, there is no way to protect savings from confiscation through inflation. There is no safe store of value."

Balloon Loan

A balloon loan is a kind of loan that does not divide its payments up evenly throughout the life of the loan. These kinds of loans are not fully amortized over the loan's term. As a result of this, one time balloon payments are mandatory at the end of the loan's time frame in order to pay off the loan's remaining principal balance.

Balloon loans have their advantages. They are often appealing to you if you are a short term borrower. This is because balloon loans commonly come with an interest rate that is lower than the interest rate of a longer term loan. These lower interest rates provide a benefit of extremely low interest payments. This leads to not only lower payments throughout the loan, but also incredibly low outlays of capital in the life span of the loan. Because the majority of the loan repayment is put off until the loan payment period's conclusion, a borrower gains great flexibility in using the capital that is freed up for the term of the loan.

The downsides to these balloon loans only surface when the borrower lacks discipline or falls victim to higher interest rates later on. If a borrower does not possess focused and consistent discipline in getting ready for the large last payment, then the individual may run into trouble at the end of the loan. This is because substantial payments along the way are not being collected. Besides this, if a borrower will be forced to engage in refinancing towards the end, then the borrower may suffer from a higher interest rate on the balloon payment that is rolled forward.

Some balloon loans also include a higher interest rate reset feature later in the life of the loan. This further exposes a borrower to the risk of higher interest rates. This is common with five year types of balloon mortgages. When a reset of the interest rate feature is present at the conclusion of the five year period, then the interest rate will be adjusted to the current rates. The amortization schedule will then be recalculated dependent on a final term of the loan. Balloon options that do not include these reset options, and many that do reset, generally encourage the loan holder to sell the property in advance of the conclusion of the original term of the loan. Otherwise, many borrowers will simply choose to refinance the loan before this point arrives.

The reasons that you might choose to get a balloon loan are several. A person who does not plan to hold onto a house or property for a long period of time would benefit from such a loan arrangement. This individual would plan to resell the house in advance of the loan expiration. Another reason for taking a balloon loan is in a refinancing. Finally, if a person anticipates a significant cash settlement or lump sum award, then they might take on a balloon loan. Commercial property owners often like balloon loans for the purchase of commercial properties as well.

Balloon loans are sometimes called balloon notes or bullet loans.

Banco Santander

Banco Santander is the largest Spanish banking group in the world. This giant financial institution boasts over 121 million customers among its various divisions. Founded in 1856, it maintains a staff of over 193,000 employees. For 2015, the group boasted a nearly six billion euros profit and a market capitalization of over 65.5 billion euros.

Banco Santander and the entire Santander Group is successful because it has a geographically diverse range in its top ten national markets. The group commands significant market shares in each of these countries. They are Spain, Germany, Portugal, Poland, Great Britain, Brazil, Mexico, Argentina, Chile, and the United States. The bank also controls important market shares in Puerto Rico and Uruguay. Its consumer finance business gives it a major reach into a number of other countries in Europe. It has exposure to China from both its consume finance and wholesale businesses.

Banco Santander operates a number of global divisions for business and consumer banking customers. These include Commercial Banking, Global Wholesale Banking, Santander Asset Management, Santander Private Banking, Santander Insurance, and Santander Cards. These groups all work together to help the Spanish financial services conglomerate satisfy its customer needs throughout the globe.

Retail banking and business customers receive financial services and products from Banco Santander's commercial banking division. They also employ their extensive commercial networks and their online services to locally distribute their wide range of services and products to customers of all kinds. This way the global business divisions are able to reach out to the group's over 100 million customers.

The Global Wholesale Banking division provides the group's extensive services and products to large corporations, institutions, and customers with particular needs. These groups require value added products and specially personalized service.

Santander Asset Management delivers investments and savings products on a global scale. These are distributed effectively via the Banco Santander commercial branch networks. In order to provide for the diverse needs of its customer base, the SAM incorporates a large range of investment products. These include pension plans, investment funds, and portfolio options. Money which is placed into these vehicles the group invests in a wide range of locations and assets types.

Banco Santander Private Banking focuses specifically on the customers who are high income throughout the globe. It delivers both asset management and personal financial advice to these individuals. This division runs from locations in Spain, Italy, the United Kingdom, and Latin America. It also supports private domestic banking operations throughout the nations of Latin America and Portugal. This sub group works with locally based commercial banks to jointly manage these special operations.

Santander Insurance is a large and impressive division. It delivers insurance protection and savings vehicles in 20 different countries to its more than 17 million customers. The group employs multi channel distribution networks to provide segmented insurance. This model is global in nature but local in its customer appeal and commercial network reach. It focuses on superior service, quality, and efficiency while working with low risk profile customers whenever possible.

Banco Santander Credit Cards is another global and significant division. The business provides payment processing services to a variety of businesses. It handles both credit and debit cards. As such the credit card division manages fully 110 million different cards throughout 16 nations. This important division comprises 11% of all the gross margin for the group. It utilizes a cutting edge and constantly changing technology and platform to standardize the risk and provide effective training and management for its employees and business customers.

Bank for International Settlements (BIS)

The Bank for International Settlements proves to be the oldest entity in the world for international financial organization. Central banks of the world established this bank on May 17 of 1930. Today 60 different central banks are members of this bank of central banks. Their economies represent 95% of all the combined Gross Domestic Product of the globe.

This Bank for International Settlements is also known by its acronym the BIS. It has an elegant mission. The goals of this organization are to help out the member central banks as they seek out financial and monetary stability, to serve as the bank for central banks, and to promote international financial cooperation in achieving stability. World headquarters for the BIS are located in Basel, Switzerland. The group also maintains two other important representative regional offices. These are in Hong Kong the Special Administrative Region of China for Asia-Pacific and in Mexico City for the Americas.

The two regional representative offices are hubs for the various BIS activities. They work to encourage cooperation between the region's central banks, supervisory authorities, and the BIS itself. This is why these offices promote data and information exchange, help to set up seminars and meetings, and provide information on the economic and financial research for the Americas and Asia.

Another important role of the Bank for International Settlements lies in its banking services. These two regional offices assist with delivering such services to the Americas and Asia-Pacific regions. Officers routinely visit the member central banks' reserve managers as part of this mission. In its Asian office it maintains a treasury dealing room for the region that offers daily trading functions for regional central banks.

The BIS set up its regional Representative Office of the Americas back in November of 2002 in Mexico City. The goal was to increase the Americas regional activities of the bank in better coordination with the headquarters office in Switzerland. They also established the Consultative Council for the Americas back in May of 2008. This advising committee helps the board of directors for the BIS to better understand the issues in the Americas region. Members of this council include central bank governors from the Americas' region member central banks. This includes the U.S., Peru, Mexico, Colombia, Chile, Canada, Brazil, and Argentina.

The bank founded its increasingly important regional Asian office on July 11 of 1998 in Hong Kong as the Representative Office for Asia and the Pacific. It acts as an area forum for economic and monetary research that is useful for the central banks and provides the regional central banks with the settlement and exchange banking services.

Improving cooperation among the various member central banks in the Asian region is another important function. This office also maintains the Asian Consultative Council. The group is comprised of central bank governors from the Asia-Pacific region member central banks. Its members include Thailand, Singapore, the Philippines, New Zealand, Malaysia, Korea, Japan, Indonesia, India, Hong Kong, China, and Australia.

The Bank for International Settlements is different from other banks in the world in several important aspects. All of its customers are either international organizations or central banks. They do not open accounts for international companies or private individuals. The BIS does not offer any financial or advisory services to any investors or corporations. It also does not take in deposits from or make loans to parties that are not central banks or international organizations. The bank does make some of its research available at no cost to companies and members of the public.

Bank Notes

A bank note refers to a promissory note that can be negotiated by the bank which issues it. The holders of such bank notes will be paid on demand. The face of the note in question states the amount which is payable. As with coins, bank notes represent legal tender. They make up the modern forms of money along with coins. These bank notes are also called simply notes, or bills.

In past times throughout Europe, Great Britain, and the United States, bank notes could be redeemed for such precious metals as silver (Great Britain and the U.S.) and gold (Europe, Great Britain, and the U.S.). They have also been exchangeable into financial assets like bank-issued bonds. Since the United States abandoned the gold standard under then-President Richard Nixon in 1971, bills are no longer redeemable for gold.

These bank notes only have legal tender transaction value at all today because the government backs them by the good faith and trust in the United States government and Treasury. Despite the facts that such notes are essentially worthless and only have value because people choose to believe in them, these bills are utilized every day around the world in literally billions of financial transactions. This means that for better or worse, bank notes are both money and currency, at least for as long as consumers continue to believe in the fiat money system (that states money can be created out of thin air by central banks).

Before bank notes arose as a form of payment, individuals and businesses throughout all of human history paid for their services and goods using other stores of tangible value, mostly in the form of precious metals like gold and silver. Banks were the earliest organizations which came up with the idea of issuing bills to represent the precious metals in a more convenient and safe to transport format.

Governments later followed suit and began to provide such notes as a means to exchange them in transactions or to redeem them at bank windows for silver or gold. The paper had no value whatsoever, but it stood as a symbol of value. The certificates which were sometimes known as silver certificates of gold certificates proved to be far more practical to carry around in bulk since they were considerably smaller and lighter.

Around that time, governments shrewdly learned that they could debase their currencies by minting coins with base metals in place of the old silver and gold pieces like Spanish silver, $20 gold pieces, and British gold and silver sovereigns. Individuals began to carry around a combination of money in the form of both paper bills and base metals coins from the mid 20th century.

Once the United States abandoned the gold standard, the other countries of the world followed suit. The notes may no longer be exchanged for silver and gold as they could for hundreds of years. They may still be converted into other kinds of assets which are financially valuable. Economists call this financial convertibility. Money that is not convertible physically still has value in theory. This is true while the central banks and commercial banks have the assets to support them and keep the system going.

In the U.S., it is the Federal Reserve Bank that carries the responsibility of regulating the quantity of currency both created and distributed. The Bureau of Printing and Engraving creates this form of money literally today. Once upon a time in the United States, commercial banks had the ability to issue banknotes alongside the U.S. Treasury. Today only the Federal Reserve Bank is permitted to create such notes in the United States. National central banks issue the bank notes which come from different countries.

Each bank note clearly denotes its value. The bills include a number of tough security features which help to decrease the chances of forgery. Despite this, there are still countless examples of bank note forgery on every continent and most countries around the world.

Bank of England

The Bank of England is the prestigious and incredibly old central bank for the United Kingdom. The country founded this model central bank in 1694 to promote the good of the individuals in the U.K. through maintaining both monetary as well as financial stability. The bank is often affectionately referred to as the "Old Lady" of Threadneedle Street.

The bank of England carries out the first part of its mission of maintaining monetary stability quite literally. Not only does it bear responsibility for keeping up the public's confidence in the national bank notes. It also literally designs, makes, and issues into circulation these quality and durable bank notes with state of the art security features. These help insure the pound sterling notes are resistant against counterfeiting efforts and are simple to check.

This role extends to safeguarding the value of the notes through time. It enables businesses and consumers to save, plan, invest, and spend their pound notes confidently. The Bank carries out this crucial role of keeping up the confidence in the notes via its monetary stability goal.

They do this by ensuring stable, low prices throughout the broad spectrum of goods and services sold around the United Kingdom. The government has defined stable prices as those which include an inflation rate of two percent year on year as demonstrated by the Consumer Prices Index. The decisions to meet this objective of inflation targeting are made in the Bank of England's Monetary Policy Committee, the MPC.

The financial crisis of 2008 demonstrated that price stability by itself will not guarantee all-around economic stability. The second mandate of the bank is to ensure financial stability. This means public confidence and belief in the important financial markets, institutions, infrastructures, and total system. Since the financial crisis, the Bank gained a few critical additional responsibilities to help it provide financial stability to the U.K.

The first of these new powers is the Bank of England's PRA Prudential Regulation Authority. This allows it to encourage financial soundness and safety of the many crucial financial firms in this global banking center. The PRA supervises and now regulates around 1,700 different banks, credit unions, building societies, insurance companies, and major investment companies.

The second new authority is the Bank of England FPC Financial Policy Committee. This is intended to enhance and safeguard the stability of the British financial system in total. They strive to ameliorate or remove altogether the risks to the overall system. This task centers on stopping financial crises in the future, or at the least lessening their severity and frequencies.

Besides these important roles, the Bank of England has a few other tasks to foster financial stability. They provide the services of market maker and lender of last resort when there is financial stress in the system. They monitor and regulate the important clearing, payment, and settlement systems in Britain. They also labor to calmly wind down any financial institutions which are failing.

Some might feel that the many responsibilities of the bank are too vast and wide ranging. The Bank of England is confident in the advantages of doing them all under the roof of one institution. The various responsibilities and tasks need a common set of analyses, information, and skills to complete.

Many of the competing objectives have common interconnections between them. These need rapid, capable, and efficient management and decision making regarding any of the conflicting trade-offs. This makes it the ultimate task of the bank to carry out each of these roles by laboring with capable coordination. It helps the Bank of England to maximize the effectiveness of its various policies to carry out their single mission of promoting the good of the people of the U.K.

Bank of Japan

The Bank of Japan is the name of the central bank in Japan. The Bank of Japan Act established this entity. Unlike a number of central banks, Japan's central bank is neither a private corporation nor a government agency.

The bank has several key objectives. These are to create and issue the country's banknotes, to handle monetary and currency control, and to guarantee the normal settlement of funds between banks and financial institutions. They do this to help maintain the financial system's stability in Japan.

The Bank of Japan Act gives the central bank its mandate for monetary and currency control. It is intended to help them achieve stability of prices so that the economy is able to develop normally. In January 2013, the bank began to interpret this price stability to be an inflation target of two percent. This means that they are looking for a change in the year over year consumer price index by a plus two percent increase. While they are committed to reaching this level of inflation as soon as they can, the bank has not yet succeeded.

Price stability is important to the Bank of Japan because they feel it is critical as a basis for the economic activity of the country. They state that as prices change significantly, it is difficult for companies and consumers to make the right investment and consumption choices. Unstable prices are also negative for fair income distribution.

To make the decisions on its monetary policy, the Bank of Japan holds eight Monetary Policy Meetings (MPMs) each year. Here the policy board considers the financial and economic situation in Japan and then chooses what money market operations they should pursue. All decisions are made by the majority vote of the nine members on the Policy Board.

The board is comprised of the Governor, two Deputy Governors, and six remaining members. Following each MPM, the bank releases to the public an assessment of prices and economic activity. They also divulge the monetary policy of the bank for that point and for the near future. This comes out with their guideline for money market operations.

The guideline that they decide on and release at the MPMs determines how many funds they will allow in the money market using their money market operations. The bank engages in funds-supplying operations by making loans to the country's financial institutions. These are backed up by the collateral the banks submit to the central bank. Opposite transactions called funds-absorbing operations occur as the Bank of Japan issues and sells government debt in the form of bills.

In the Financial Crisis of 2008, the central bank chose three areas in which to expand monetary policy to help stabilize the economy and encourage economic expansion. They began by reducing their policy interest rate. They next took appropriate measures to make sure that Japanese markets had financial stability. As part of this effort, the Bank of Japan restarted purchasing bank stocks. It also engaged in offering additional loans to banks at subordinated interest rates.

Finally, the bank took various steps to facilitate struggling corporate financing. They created and designated special funds and operations to encourage lending to corporations in Japan. They also expanded the variety of collateral they would accept for corporate debt. For a year, they even purchased company's commercial paper and corporate bonds in an effort to help companies find the financing they needed for normal operations.

The bank has also engaged in quantitative easing, creating money and using it to buy assets of banks and companies that needed support. They continue to pursue these policies in an effort to encourage growth and inflation in their economy.

Bank Run

A bank run is an event that happens when a bank or financial institution's customers choose to withdraw all of their deposits at the same time. This happens because of fears of the solvency of a particular bank. The effect is like a snowball. The more individuals who pull out their funds the greater the default probability becomes. This in turn leads still other customers to pull out their deposits. Severe bank run cases can create a scenario where the reserves of the bank are insufficient to meet all withdrawal demands.

Bank runs like these are not usually a result of actual insolvency of a financial institution. Rather they occur because of panic. Such fear can still evolve into a self fulfilling prophecy as a greater number of clients request their money. What starts as rumor and panic can transform into an actual ugly insolvency scenario. This means the fear of a default can actually cause a default in banking circles.

Banks run into these troubling situations sometimes because they generally only hold a tiny percentage of their actual deposits at hand. When withdrawal demands rise, it forces banks to boost their cash reserves. A common method for doing this is to sell assets, often at fire sale prices because they need funds immediately. The losses banks book for selling off assets at greatly reduced prices can lead them to actual insolvency. A bank run can become a full scale bank panic when a number of banks experience such runs on them all at once.

The best known example of a bank run occurred surrounding the infamous stock market crash in 1929. This led to numerous runs on financial institutions throughout the United States and finally to the Great Depression. The cascade of runs on the banks in the end of 1929 and the beginning of 1930 became like dominos falling. One bank's failure created fear and caused the panic of customers at neighboring banks that motivated them to take out their deposits as well. A failing bank in Nashville at the time created a number of bank runs throughout the Southeastern U.S.

Still other runs on banks occurred in the Great Depression because of the rumors begun by individual clients of the banks. The Bank of United States told a New York customer in December of 1930 he should not sell a certain stock he held. He departed from the branch and told other customers and individuals that the bank could not or would not sell his stock shares. Clients of the bank thought this meant the bank was insolvent. Thousands of them then lined up and withdrew more than $2 million out of the bank in only hours.

The developed nations' governments enacted a serious of steps to decrease the possibilities for future date bank runs as a result of the chaos in the 1930s. The most effective centered on minimum bank reserve requirements. These dictated what percent of aggregate deposits banks had to keep readily available in cash.

In 1933, the American Congress also created the FDIC Federal Deposit Insurance Corporation. They established it as a direct result of the numerous bank failures. The government agency has since then insured deposits in banks to a maximum account amount. It works to keep up public confidence and banking stability within the financial system of the United States.

Bank Stress Tests

Bank stress tests are special analyses that a government authority or company runs to determine the strength of a bank to resist difficult economic times. They conduct such tests using economic conditions that are unfavorable to learn if the banks possess sufficient capital to survive the effects of negative financial environments. In the United States, the law requires that banks which claim at least $50 billion worth of assets must perform their own internal stress tests. Their risk management department is responsible for overseeing these. The Federal Reserve conducts these stress tests on such banks as well.

The idea behind these bank stress tests is to look at several critical risks which can afflict the banks and banking system. They are supposed to evaluate the financial condition of the bank being tested in one or more crisis scenarios with regards to liquidity risk, market risk, and credit risk. The tests simulate fictitious potential crises using a number of different factors that the International Monetary Fund and Federal Reserve determine.

This mostly came about after the worldwide financial crisis and Great Recession of 2007-2009. As many banks had failed or nearly collapsed, government and international bodies became more concerned about checking on the financial strength of banks in potential crisis scenarios.

These bank stress tests were effectively set up and used on a widespread basis after this worst collapse since the Great Depression of the 1930s. The financial crisis had left in its wake a number of financial institutions, investment banks, and commercial banks that had insufficient capital. The stress tests were established to deal with this threat before it became severely problematic again.

There are two main types of bank stress tests that exist. The Federal Reserve runs its own yearly oversight stress tests of the U.S. banks that have at least $50 billion in assets on their balance sheets. The primary purpose of such a stress test is to learn if the banks possess sufficient capital to weather the storm of challenging economic conditions.

The company operated stress tests are done twice a year by law. They must be strictly reported according to the deadlines set by the Fed. Results must be turned in to the Federal Reserve board by no later than January 5th and July 5th.

In either of the stress tests, the banks receive a typical set of circumstances to evaluate their performance. It might be a 30% free fall in the prices of housing, a 5% to 10% decline in the stock market, and a 10% or higher unemployment rate. The banks must then take their future nine quarters of financial forecasts to ascertain if their capital levels are sufficient to endure the hypothetical crisis.

These bank stress tests have broader repercussions. Banks must make public their results by publishing them after they undergo the tests. The pubic and investors then learn how the bank in question would survive in a significant crisis situation. Laws and regulations passed since the financial crisis require that companies which are unable to pass the stress tests must cut their share buyback programs and dividend payments so that they can preserve the capital they have.

There are cases where banks receive a conditional passing grade on a stress test. This result states that the bank nearly failed its test. It puts them at risk of not being allowed to engage in more capital distributions going forward. Conditional passing means that a bank has to turn in a plan of action to address the capital shortfall.

These failures cause a bank to look bad to not only investors but the banking public. There have been a number of banks that failed such stress tests. Foreign banks like Germany's Deutsche Bank and Spain's Santander have failed to pass such tests on a number of occasions.

Barings Bank Collapse

The Barings Bank collapse is a tale of tragedy involving greed, poor banking oversight, and a complete failure of internal checks and balances that ruined the oldest bank in London and banker to the Queen. It took only several weeks for Nick Leeson the Singapore trading head of the bank to amass hundreds of millions of pounds in losses which he camouflaged as profits before fleeing from the law. After the family led management uncovered how severe the losses were, the bank went into bankruptcy protection until the Dutch banking giant ING acquired it for only a single pound.

Barings had originally been founded by brothers John, Charles, and Francis Baring on Christmas of 1762. The company started out as a merchant firm but quickly began to finance other merchants as a true bank. The bank gained fame over the years for financing many historic events. It helped the British government pay for the Revolutionary War in America and then the Napoleonic Wars in France. The bank financed the Louisiana Purchase for America in 1803 so that the fledgling country could double the size of U.S. for $15 million. In 1806, Barings moved to its Bishopsgate office in London which remained its headquarters for nearly 200 years until the Barings Bank collapse.

The banker to Queen Elizabeth had grown its commercial activities successfully for centuries. It floated the renowned Guinness brewery in 1886 and expanded its commercial endeavors after barely surviving collapse through a Bank of England bailout because of an Argentina near debt default. The bank eventually bought a Japanese based securities firm in 1984. In 1991 it obtained a 40 percent stake in Dillon Read the U.S. investment bank.

The negative turning point for the bank came after they put Nick Leeson in charge of Barings Futures Singapore (BFS) in 1992. He had come over from Morgan Stanley three years before as a banker in the back office. His unit's function centered on only trading futures contracts for customers on the Nikkei 225 and 10 year Japanese bonds. The mistake came in putting Leeson in charge of both the transaction settlement operations and the trading floor. At the time, James Bax the head of Barings' Asia lamented that the structure they were setting up would lead to both a loss of a huge amount of money and customer goodwill.

Barings Bank collapse was brought on by the BFS group starting to trade with its own account. Leeson was attempting to gain from arbitrage spreads between Singapore and Japanese exchanges. The London management and chairman Peter Baring believed that this was extremely profitable and basically risk free trading. The problems arose from Leeson establishing a secret account called 88888 where he began to make enormous bets on Japanese markets.

At first he appeared to make the company huge amounts of money, including 10 million pounds in 1993 that represented 10% of all the bank's annual profits. In 1995, the secret account was uncovered, along with losses of 827 million pounds he had wracked up in the name of Barings in only a matter of weeks. Leeson had left a note that said "I'm sorry" in the Singapore office and gone on the run.

Once he was captured and extradited back to Asia, Singapore charged him with fraud and forgery. They sentenced him to jail where he spent four years. Leeson later emerged from prison and sold his story as an autobiography Rogue Trader and the rights to the movie of the same title.

As a result of the Barings Bank collapse, the Bank of England lost banking oversight powers that were given to the newly organized Financial Services Authority. This organization later received criticism for ineffectively overseeing the banks under its charge and making the 2008 financial crisis significantly worse. The name Barings ceased to exist except in an asset management arm that an American life insurance group purchased. The bank's collapse ended the longest running and most famous banking dynasty in the world.

Ben Bernanke

Ben Bernanke served as Chairman of the Federal Reserve System's Board of Governors from February 1, 2006 until January 31, 2014. As the successor to former Chairman Alan Greenspan, Bernanke received his Congressional approval because of his expertise in the failed monetary policies led to the Great Depression and for his ideology of targeting inflation.

Bernanke left many legacies from his eight year term in the office. When the banking and financial crises broke out, he developed many ground breaking and unprecedented Federal Reserve tools to stave off a worldwide financial depression.

Ben Bernanke also took the Fed into unchartered territories with bailouts of global insurance giant AIG (to the tune of $150 billion) and investment bank Bear Stearns. In order to prevent a global banking panic, Bernanke's Fed chose to loan out $540 billion to the money market funds so they could meet the overwhelming liquidation requests from their customers.

Ben Bernanke expanded his and the Fed's roles in growing the group's open market operations after they found lowered interest rates were not enough to close out the destabilizing financial crisis of 2008. He created the infamous American quantitative easing programs and Operation Twist as part of these efforts. Critics constantly accused him of playing with hyperinflationary fire, but Bernanke insisted that the dangers primarily lay in doing too little and not too much to save the economy.

After Ben Bernanke resigned from his important position as Chairman of the Fed at the end of January 2014, his Vice Chair Janet Yellen succeeded him as the new Fed Chairman. Yellen had demonstrated in the past that she agreed with many of his policies. Bernanke then went on to become a member of the Economic Studies Program at Brookings Institute where he was appointed as a Distinguished Fellow in Residence. He is also an affiliate of the Hutchins Center on Fiscal and Monetary Policy. Here he helps to analyze and educate members of the public regarding monetary and fiscal policies.

Ben Bernanke's efforts to guide monetary policy in the American economy yielded results at a difficult time for the nation. The national debt's growth had severely limited fiscal policy over the past decade. Bernanke served as the nation's leading economic expert as the spokesman and public face of the Federal Reserve. His speeches continuously influenced the dollar's value against other currencies and gold as well as the American stock markets. Many believe that in his time as the Chairman of the Fed, big Ben Bernanke evolved into the most critical single individual in the U.S. and worldwide economies.

Ben Bernanke set a number of records while Chairman of the Fed. Other chairman had only previously used the Fed funds rate to reduce inflation or stop recessions. Ben also utilized this critical national lending rate, employing rate cuts on ten separate occasions from September of 2007 to December of 2008. During this time, he conclusively reduced the interest rate from 5.25% to 0%. When this by itself did not prove sufficient to rebuild liquidity in sinking and panicked banks, Bernanke relaxed banking reserve requirements, reduced the discount borrowing rate, and eventually provided credit to the banks via the discount window, something else that had never been done. This still did not thaw the lending freeze.

Bernanke then developed and launched the TAF Term Auction Facility in December of 2007. With this program, Bernanke and company loaned literally billions of dollars to banks in exchange for their notorious bad debts as collateral for the loans. The TAF turned out to not be so temporary as intended. It expanded until it reached an enormous $1 trillion amount by June of 2008.

As credit markets around the world had frozen up, Bernanke labored with other major central bank heads globally to restore lost liquidity. His contribution to this important effort included increasing the dollar credit swap lines by $180 billion. By injecting trillions of dollars into the U.S. and global economies, Bernanke earned the scornful nickname of "Helicopter Ben" from his detractors who were convinced his proverbial throwing money out of helicopters would lead to national hyperinflation in the end.

Blanket Loans

Blanket loans are those which cover multiple properties or parcels of land. They handle the costs for or can be secured by more than a single piece of real estate. These are most typically employed by commercial land developers or investors. For individual consumers, they can be utilized as a type of bridge between new and old properties and mortgages. For these consumers, such a blanket loan will make it possible to pay for both mortgages until the owner reaches the point of selling the old property.

The feature that makes these mortgages most useful for developers is their release clause. These permit the borrowers to sell a single or even several pieces of real estate without the need of being forced to refinance the mortgage. This makes them significantly different from traditional mortgages. Normal mortgages make borrowers completely pay down their loan balance before they can sell the property which secures them.

For developers of residential properties, they find these blanket loans particularly helpful. They employ them to pay for large tracts of land on which they will build. When it is time for the loan to fund, it becomes secured by the full piece of property. The developer is allowed to subdivide his property and sell it in individual lots. For part of the security to be released, the developer must utilize some of the sale proceeds to pay down part of the loan.

This is helpful when builders are constructing subdivisions. Such a developer could put the blanket loan to use to buy the consecutive pieces of land while they are available. The developer would then be able to subdivide the total land into specific lots for building houses. With each home that he finishes and sells, the property becomes detached from the blanket loan without the financing having to be disrupted on the remainder of the development project.

Consumers also find these types of blanket loans helpful in making it possible to transition from the sale of their current home to the building or buying of the new house. This makes much more sense than having two concurrent mortgages or obtaining a more costly short term bridge loan. It can also help them so that they do not have to sell the property early and move into a rental while they look for a property to purchase.

These kinds of blanket loans are often governed by a contingency clause. These clauses detail that the newly purchased house and its mortgage will not close until the person is able to sell the existing home. The problem with such a contingency clause is that they have limited time frames on them. They may force a borrower into selling the home in a panic in order to meet the clause expiration date. This can lead to a lower selling price or disadvantageous terms on the sale.

Blanket loans get around such a dilemma by providing the borrowers with an extended period of time in the clause to sell their old house. Sometimes they are arranged as interest payment only loans for a full 12 months before amortizing starts. This gives the seller a sufficient time period to sell the house for a good price and reduces the overall burden of the mortgage at the same time.

The main downside to blanket loans for individuals is that they are significantly harder to find since the real estate crash and Great Recession of 2009. Their advantages include both flexibility and efficiency in financing. For an individual consumer, this means a single mortgage payment rather than two. Developers do not have to worry about constantly refinancing their property debt as they sell off parts of the property. Should a developer default on his loan, the bank simply assumes control of all remaining property which secures the loan.

BNP Paribas

BNP Paribas is the largest French-based bank in the world. It has strong roots in the banking history of Europe. Today it remains one of the leading banks on the continent and Euro zone as well as an important international banking group. The group claims 189,000 employees around the world, of which the overwhelming majority of 146,610 are based in Europe.

It also has an extensive international network of branches and employees. The bank maintains 19,845 employees in America; 12,180 workers in Asia; 9,860 staff members in Africa; and 580 employees in the Middle East, as of 2015. BNP Paribas locations can be found in 75 different countries and territories around the world. For 2015, it boasted 42.9 billion euros of revenue and 6.7 billion euros of net profit.

The bank organizes itself along two main business lines. These are Retail Banking and Services (RBS) and the Corporate Institutional Banking (CIB) divisions. The Retail Banking & Services division covers its retail banking activities and specialized financial products and services in both France and the rest of the world. The company subdivides this into Domestic Markets and International Financial Services.

The group's Domestic Markets is comprised of the company's four retail banking networks found in the euro zone, as well as three specific lines of business. The retail bank networks are FRB French Retail Banking located in France, BNP Paribas Fortis in Belgium, BNL in Italy, and BGL BNP Paribas found in Luxembourg. Its three specific business lines are Arval the long term corporate leasing program, its Leasing Solutions that provide financing and rental services, and its Personal Investors that offer online brokerage services and savings vehicles.

Corporate clients also can access the business of Cash Management and Factoring. High Net Worth Individuals have the company's Wealth Management business as their private banking franchise within the domestic markets of the group. As of 2015, the Domestic Markets subdivision boasts over 15 million individual customers located in 27 countries. The bank also counts almost 1 million clients comprised of professional individuals, small businesses, and corporate entities. To service these numerous accounts, they devote the efforts of 68,000 employees in these over two dozen countries.

International Financial Services of the group handles the company's diversified business activities operating in over 60 countries. The group's Personal Finance provides credit to people residing in 30 countries. They deliver products and services via such major brands as Findomestic, Cofinoga, and Cetelem.

The IFS division also operates several other businesses. International Retail Banking covers the retail bank operations in another 15 non-euro zone nations like TEB in Turkey and Bank of the West in the U.S. BNP Paribas Cardif offers savings and insurance for assets, projects, and individuals living in 36 countries.

IFS rounds out its business lines with three specific asset management and private banking operations. These include the group's Wealth Management for private banking, their Investment Partners for asset management, and their BNP Paribas Real Estate for international real estate services. All of the International Financial Services businesses and lines together employ over 80,000 staff residing in over 60 countries.

The group's Corporate & Institutional Banking (CIB) prides itself on being a leading worldwide provider of financial products and services to its institutional and corporate clients around the globe. They group counts 13,000 of these clients in 57 countries throughout Europe/Middle East/Africa, the America, and Asia Pacific. To support them it maintains nearly 30,000 staff.

The company delivers specialized services that help their clients through treasury, financing, securities services, capital markets, and financial advisory offerings. It proves to be a world-renowned leader throughout numerous disciplines. As such, CIB has vast expertise in derivatives, risk management, structured financing, and other areas. The CIB division serves as a bridge between the two types of clients it counts by helping its corporate clients to obtain financing while offering investment possibilities to its institutional investors.

British Bankers Association (BBA)

The British Bankers Association turns out to be the members' representative for the biggest international banking cluster in the world. This main trade association for the British banking sector boasts over 200 member banks headquartered in both the U.K. and more than 50 other countries that run operations in over 180 jurisdictions around the globe. As such fully 80% of all the systemically critical banks on earth carry membership with the BBA. This is the voice of UK banking.

The BBA claims the greatest and most comprehensive policy resources for those banks operating in the UK. They represent membership not only to the government of the U.K., but also throughout Europe and globally. Besides this impressive membership roster, their network also is comprised of more than 80 of the foremost professional and financial services organizations in the world.

The BBA's members collectively manage over £7 trillion (British pounds) of British bank assets. The members employ almost half a million people throughout the country. Their contributions to the British economy every year are more than £60 billion. Members loan in excess of £150 billion out to business based in the U.K.

The British Bankers Association works to encourage both initiatives and policies that promote the interests of not only banks but also the overall public. They have three principal priorities in their work. The first is to help out customers. This includes both businesses and consumers. The second is to encourage growth. By this they intend to support Britain as the world's global financial center. Finally they are interested in improving standards in the industry on both an ethical and professional level.

The BBA works with two strategic aims in mind. The first is to encourage a superior and improving banking sector for the overall U.K. They do this by working alongside banks and other beneficiaries to increase trust in the banking industry, by raising standards, by encouraging growth, and by assisting customers. They promise to facilitate public approval and overall awareness of the important position banks play in the economy. They are also aspiring to build appreciation for the advantages of hosting an internationally critical banking sector.

Chief among their public relations tasks are to encourage acknowledgement of the substantial improvements the sector has gone through since the global financial crisis. The BBA's goal is to be understood as an agent of positive change that makes a better banking industry by its non members and members alike. They strive to be a trusted partner of both banking regulators and the government. They also take the initiative to impact international and national debates on banking issues.

Their second strategic aim is to be the banking industry's trade association that is world class. They are the principal trade association for the foremost sector of the British economy as well as the main trade group for the foremost banking cluster in the world. This is why they aim to be best in class in their operations.

Before September in 2012, the BBA both compiled and published the LIBOR London Interbank Offered Rate, the most important interest rate in the world. They lost their role in managing the rate after the Barclays scandal erupted that showed the bank had been consistently manipulating the rate for a number of years. As lobby organization for the rate submitting banks, the Bank of England decided the BBA's conflict of interest was too great.

Nowadays the BBA puts on training and events throughout Britain. These include training classes, briefings, and forums besides their annual industry dinners and conferences. They also publish a monthly report that covers figures on high street banking. This is used in their Annual Abstract of Banking Statistics that they produce every August. BBA furthermore runs the GOLD Global Operational Loss Database for members. This serves as a helpful tool in helping to manage risk from operations.

Bundesbank

The central bank of Germany is the Deutsche Bundesbank. The Federal Republic of Germany established it as the German central bank in 1957. The bank headquarters reside in Frankfurt in the state of Main. The bank maintains regional offices throughout nine cities in the country. These regional offices have a total of 35 different branches.

This bank is different from many central banks in its many locations and interactions with the public. The Bundesbank has a presence in every major region of Germany. Every regional office has responsibility for either one federal state or sometimes several of them.

The Bundesbank Executive Board makes the decisions for the central bank. The President of the bank, Vice President, and other members comprise this critical body.

The Bundesbank carries out a number or roles. It provides the German economy with bank notes. The bank is also the regulator for supervising the German banks. Besides traditional central banking roles like these, it also provides information to the public in the form of economic education through its around 40 locations in the country. About 2,600 staff work in the regional offices. Another approximately 2,600 employees serve in the branches of the bank.

Bundesbank branches and regional locations have different roles. The regional offices prove to be the on-site financial institution supervisors. Each of the regional offices is responsible to oversee the financial services and banks that operate in their one or more regions. These supervisors have to consider and evaluate reports and notifications that the banks must submit in turn routinely. Among these is their statement of annual accounts.

The supervisors from the regional offices of the central bank also have regular meetings with these financial institutions' senior management teams. Inspectors from the regional office determine if the liquidity and capital on hand are sufficient according to the laws. They also decide if the banks are meeting the minimum risk handling requirements.

Assessing credit is another critical role that the regional office staff carry out with the individual banks. They provide the banks with money in exchange for collateral the central bank accepts as eligible. Regional offices make sure that the balance sheets are healthy.

Economic education comes from the regional offices as well. Experts from the central bank give updates in plain language on important issues like monetary policy, cash, and financial markets. They do this at events held in each region, like the "Bundesbank Forum." Any member of the public is allowed to attend. Regional offices also provide seminars to students and teacher on developments in monetary policy.

Branches of the central bank are where matters related to cash are handled in the country. These branches issue the new banknotes and coins into circulation by delivering them to the major customers such as grocery stores and financial institutions. The branches are responsible for checking deposited coins and banknotes to make sure they are authentic and of high quality. They replace damaged ones for any customer who brings them to the branch.

In order for a customer to exchange a bank note, he or she must have minimally 50% of the note in hand. If they do not, customers must offer conclusive proof that the missing part of the note was destroyed.

Germany's central bank does not set interest rates or conduct monetary policy on its own. As a member of the euro zone, the country has ceded control of this important function to the European Central Bank. The German central bank is an important member of the ECB and plays a major role in influencing the overall policy of the euro zone wide central bank.

Citigroup

By number of countries and territories in which it operates as well as raw numbers of customers, Citigroup is the largest global bank. The United States based banking giant offers a substantial variety of financial products and services to its 100 million individual, corporate, institutional, and government customers around the world. The bank maintains a presence in more than 100 countries and territories throughout the globe. It operates in two primary groups of the Global Consumer Bank and the Institutional Clients Group.

Citigroup's Global Consumer Bank offers services throughout the most rapidly expanding cities in 24 different countries around the world. This group boasts over 100 million individual customers. Within the Global Consumer Bank (GCB), Citi runs four geographically based business lines in their four regions of North America, Latin America, Asia, and Europe/Middle East/Africa.

These are Retail Banking, Commercial Banking, Retail Services, and Branded Credit Cards. The Citi GCB boasts over a century of well-respected market leadership and brand recognition throughout areas such as the United States, Mexico, and Asia. It is focused on expanding its high credit profiled customer base utilizing its global abilities and reach.

The Institutional Clients Group operates in over 100 countries. It is here that Citigroup is able to assist multinational corporations in expanding, hiring, providing services, and delivering products. Citi proudly offers finance capabilities and support to not only companies, but also governments at every level. It assists them not only in funding their daily operations, but also in creating sustainable transportation, housing, infrastructure, schools, and other key public works and services.

Institutional investors are able to maximize the depth of product offerings and global footprint to reach into both local and international markets. Citigroup boasts an impressive history of financing among the most transforming projects in the world during the last two centuries. They remain devoted to supporting expansion and creative innovation around the world today with cash management, lending, and advisory services.

The Citigroup ICG maintains trading floors in over 80 nations, as well as custody and clearing networks in more than 60 countries and has connections via 400 different clearing systems. This means that Citi proudly controls among the biggest global financial facilities and infrastructure platforms. These help it to facilitate the movement of a daily average of more than $3 trillion in global monetary flows.

The ICG Group if Citigroup operates six primary businesses. Citi's Capital Markets Origination business concentrates on raising capital for their institutional clients. This includes cross border issues, transactions, and exchanges.

The Citigroup Corporate and Investment Banking business delivers complete relationship coverage and service utilizing product, sector, and nation expertise to provide their worldwide abilities to clients in whichever market they wish to have a competitive presence. They organize these teams by country and industry. Every team is comprised of the two parts. Strategic Coverage Officers provides for merger and acquisition and equity financing activities. Corporate Bankers work with the Global Subsidiaries Group and Citi Capital Markets in order to help provide finance and banking services to local, national, regional, and global customers.

Citi's Markets and Securities Services business delivers world-leading financial services and products to its thousands of institutions, investors, corporations, and government clients. It covers an impressive array of asset classes, sectors, currencies, and products. Among these products are commodities, equities, futures, credit, emerging markets, foreign exchange, G10 rates, prime finance, municipals, and securitized markets.

The Citigroup Global Private Bank business is a world leader. They have 800 private bankers residing in 16 countries at 51 individual offices who provide dependable advice to members of the most successful families and influential private individuals on earth.

Finally, the Citigroup Treasury and Trade Solutions, or TTS, business delivers trade finance and seamless cash management services to Citi's wide range of financial institutions, multinational corporations, and public sector outfits throughout the world. These services include receivables, payments, investment services, liquidity management services, commercial card programs, working capital solutions, and trade finance.

Compound Interest

Compound interest represents interest which calculates on both the original principal amount as well as the interest that was accumulated previously during the loan or investment. Economists have called this miraculous phenomenon an interest on interest. It causes loans or invested deposits to increase at a significantly faster pace than only simple interest, the opposite of compound interest. Simple interest proves to be interest that calculates on just the principal amount of money.

Compound interest accrues at an interest rate which determines how often the compounding occurs. The higher the compound interest rate turns out to be, the faster the principal will compound and the more compounding periods will occur. Consider an example of how effective compounding truly is. $100 that is compounded at a rate of 10% per year will turn out to be less than $100 which is compounded at only 5% but semi annually during the same length of time.

Compound interest is important to individuals as it is able to take a few dollars worth of savings now and transform them into significant money throughout lifetimes. Investors do not need an MBA or a Wall Street background in order to benefit from this principle. Practically all investments earn compounding interest if the owners leave these earnings in the investment account over the long term.

This form of interest cuts both ways on the receiving and paying sides. When individuals are saving and investing money, it helps them grow the amount faster. When they are borrowing and paying the same interest on the debt, it grows against them faster. Individuals who are saving wish their money to compound as often as they can. Individuals who are borrowing wish it to compound as infrequently as possible. Savers are better off if they are able to compound quarterly instead of annually while just the opposite is true for borrowers.

For people who are compounding their investments, time works on their side. Money that grows at a rate of 6% each year doubles every 12 years. This means that it increases to four times as much as the original amount in only 24 years. For individuals paying compound interest, time is similarly working against them. Credit card companies utilize this principle to keep their card owners in debt forever by encouraging them to only make minimum monthly payments on the bills.

Thanks to compounding, a smaller amount of money that a person adds to an account upfront is more valuable than a larger sum of money he or she adds decades later. This cuts both ways. By paying down principal on a credit card with an extra $5 per month, the amount of compound interest individuals pay on a 14% interest rate credit card decreases by $1,315 over ten years. This is true even though they have paid only $600 in extra payments over this amount of time.

Anyone can make the miracle of compounding work for them. The idea works the same whether individuals are investing $100 or $100 million instead. Millionaires have greater ranges of investment choices. Even relatively poor people can compound their interest to increase their original amount and double their money as often as possible.

Compounding interest means that participants have to give up using some dollars today in order to obtain a greater benefit from them in the future. The little money may be missed now, but the rewards for the more significant amounts in the future will more than make up for the little sacrifice the individual makes now. Financial planners have claimed that the difference between poverty and financial comfort in the future amounts to even a few dollars in savings each week invested now rather than later.

Credit Suisse

Credit Suisse is a leading global Swiss-based banking giant whose history stretches back to 1856. Their global reach is supported by operations in more than 50 different countries. This banking group maintains over 48,000 employees who hail from more than 150 different countries around the globe. Their broad international reach allows the bank to create a well-balanced revenue stream geographically and helps them to engage in significant opportunities for growth throughout the globe.

Credit Suisse serves its international clientele in three divisions which are regionally focused. These are the Swiss Universal Bank, the International Wealth Management, and the Asia Pacific divisions. The three principle divisions receive support from Global Markets and Investment Banking & Capital Markets support divisions.

The Swiss Universal Bank focuses on the home country market of Switzerland. Here Credit Suisse delivers a significant variety of financial products and services to corporate, private, and institutional clients residing generally in Switzerland. The Private Banking business here is one of the leading brands in the country.

More than 1.6 million individuals or entities count themselves as customers of this business of the bank. This includes not only regular retail clients, but also affluent and ultra high net worth individuals (HNWI). Included in this division is their Bank-now consumer finance business. This division also provides top of the line service, technology, and platform support for asset managers throughout Switzerland. The bank within Switzerland is comprised of 184 branches and 1,570 relationship managers. Included in this is their affiliate bank Neue Aargauer Bank.

The Swiss Universal Bank division also has the Corporate and Institutional Banking business. It provides best in class services and advice to over 100,000 corporations, businesses, financial institutions, and commodity traders. Included in this business is their Swiss investment banking business. This division comprises 48 different locations and 490 relationship managers.

The second Credit Suisse division is the bank's International Wealth

Management. Here they take care of international institutional, corporate, and private clients by offering them expert advice and a wide variety of financial products and services. The Private Banking business helps wealthy individual clients and outside asset managers throughout Europe, Africa, the Middle East, and Latin America.

The bank maintains 46 locations and 1,200 relationship managers. Besides their own products, they also represent a number of third party services and products. The Asset Management business provides investment products and services worldwide to governments, pension funds, endowments, foundations, individuals, and corporations. This business concentrates on both traditional as well as alternative asset allocations and strategies.

The third Credit Suisse division is the group's Asia Pacific group. Here they focus on providing financial services and products to their high net worth and ultra high net worth individual clients, as well as corporate, entrepreneur, and institutional customers. The group offers its clients integrated access and support to the wider financial markets, specific financing solutions, and numerous products.

Within this division, the Private Banking business offers tailored products and services that include digital access to the private banking services. They maintain 13 locations throughout 7 countries and 590 relationship managers within them. The Investment Banking business in this division advises their important clients on merger and acquisition deals, on takeover defense strategies and divestitures. Also on corporate restructuring and sales, and offers debt and equity underwriting services to institutions and individual and business clients.

Besides this, the Investment Banking business covers trading and sales of both equities and fixed income instruments and offers a variety of derivatives, equity and debt securities, and opportunities for financing for its sovereign, corporate, and institutional customers.

Credit Suisse's core strengths remain its leading worldwide reputation and presence as a wealth manger, its impressive market share in home country Switzerland, and its particular skills and abilities in investment banking.

Custodial Account

A Custodial Account refers to a particular type of savings account. These can be accessed via a mutual fund company, financial institution, or brokerage firm. With these accounts, an adult controls and manages the funds or assets on behalf of a minor who is less than 18 years old. State laws govern the rules that affect these special accounts. Minors may not perform transactions in such an account without first obtaining mandatory approval of the custodian. Such an account might also be one of the retirement accounts which a custodian handles for any and all employees in a firm who are eligible to have one of these.

With a Custodial Account, it is typically the guardian or parent of the minor in question who has oversight on the account. Such investments contained in these forms of accounts are limited to mutual funds or similar products that regulated investment companies offer their clients. Every company that administers such a Custodial Account will have its own particular rules on the interest rate levels and account balance minimums they maintain.

What is interesting is that any person is allowed to contribute into a Custodial Account. The minors will not have access to any choices made by the account or money in it without their guardian's consent until they attain the legal age of adult hood. At this point, the ownership of the account transfers over from the custodian(s) and on to the minor. The minor would then gain full decision-making powers over how and when to utilize this money.

Two different kinds of Custodial Accounts exist in the United States. These are the UGMA Uniform Gift to Minors Act administered accounts and the UTMA Uniform Transfers to Minors Act ones. With the UGMA, parents and other are able to provide assets to their minor children in the forms of cash, savings bonds, life insurance, annuities, or stocks. The UTMA permit parents to postpone any distributions from the account. Each state has its own age limits which can be established by the parents or guardians.

There are a number of advantages to these two types of Custodial Accounts. Withdrawal penalties, contribution limits, and income restrictions do not apply to either of them. When a single contribution in excess of $14,000 goes into the account, this does become treated as a "gift," and the IRS will naturally then levy a gift tax on the total. Custodians also have the ability to transfer the account balance over to a 529 plan. In order to do this, the custodian first will be required to close out any investments inside the account which are not cash.

There are a few disadvantages for the minors to having one of these accounts. The government and university/college systems recognize such accounts as assets. This means that they will often decrease the ability of the minor to obtain financial aid in the college or university admissions process. This is why financial planners will often suggest that such an account should not be opened for any minor who might hope to qualify to receive financial aid packages.

Taxes will also apply to withdrawals from these accounts. Every state has its own ruling on the matter regarding whether they will be taxed at the rate of the minor or the parents' income tax bracket. Some of the unearned income becomes tax free. The rest will become fully taxable at either the child's or guardian's federal tax rate. There will also be capital gains taxes assessed on any earnings from liquidated assets in these Custodial Accounts.

Any gifts presented to such an account can not be rescinded later. The beneficiary of the account also can not be changed subsequently. The parents are required by law to file the child's tax returns when they have such an account until the minor becomes old enough to transfer over the ownership of the account. Once the minor attains the age of 18, then all dividends and earnings within the account will become subject to the minor's applicable tax rate.

Deutsche Bank

Deutsche Bank is the leading German bank in the world. It commands a substantial market share in Germany, a strong place in European banking, and an important presence in both the Asia Pacific and Americas regions.

The group has grown from its founding in Berlin, Germany in 1870 to encompass strong operating bases in all of the major developed and emerging markets. This gives them a solid prospect for business expansion in the world's rapidly growing markets, comprising Lain America, Central and Eastern Europe, and the Asia Pacific regions. Their important position in Europe provides the bank with a solid foundation from which to benefit not only from the resilient economic conditions in native market Germany, but also from rebounding strong corporate activity levels throughout the euro zone.

From Deutsche Bank's first international foray into Asia in 1872 on, the bank has always looked abroad for opportunities to expand. This has carried it into more than 70 nations around the world today. Of its 2,790 total branches, 1,827 are located in Germany and another 963 are found in other countries and markets beyond the bank's home base. With the ongoing theme of continuous globalization in the international economy dominating, this puts the banking group in a strong position. It has more than adequate diversification throughout different regions of the world and significant revenue streams coming in from all the major areas around the globe.

Deutsche Bank offers practical banking solutions and services to private individuals, medium and small businesses, corporations, institutional investors, and governments. They operate a number of businesses specifically focused on the needs of these client bases.

The Corporate Finance Business group takes responsibility for M&A merger and acquisition activities. This includes equity and debt issues, advisory services, and coverage of capital markets for medium to large corporations. They deliver this complete range of financial services and products to the business clients via industry- and regional- specific teams. A subdivision of this is the CIB Corporate & Investment Banking business. It combines the expertise of Deutsche Bank's corporate finance, commercial banking, and transaction banking under the direction of a single unified leadership team. It is made up of both the Corporate Finance and Global Transaction Banking businesses.

The Deutsche Bank Private & Business Clients Corporate business offers in branch financial and banking services to self employed entrepreneurs, private clients, and medium to small businesses on an international scale.

The bank's Wealth Management business provides high quality and extremely personalized services to the ultra high and high net worth families and individuals along with certain institutions. These particular clients receive a complete package of wealth management services, philanthropic activity advisory services, and inheritance planning advice.

The Asset Management business at Deutsche Bank delivers investment and mutual fund services and products to its retail clients around the world. The bank brands this franchise as the DWS Investments group. It also provides institutional clients of the bank like insurance companies and pension funds with a wide variety of services and products that range from traditional to alternative investments. Among these products and services are the DWS Funds, Deutsch Insurance Asset Management, DB Advisors Institutional Asset Management, and RREEF Real Estate Investment Management.

Deutsche Bank also operates a large and important Asia Pacific division of the bank. The company's history in Asia traces back to the first branches they opened in Shanghai, China and Yokohama, Japan which it founded in 1872. Nowadays the operation is quite a bit larger. The group maintains office presences in 16 national markets and employs 16,000 staff in Asia Pacific. The bank's Asia Pacific division headquarters are located in Singapore.

Dodd-Frank Act

The Dodd-Frank Act is fully entitled the Dodd-Frank Wall Street Reform and Consumer Protection Act. This enormous law served to reform the financial world following the financial crisis and Great Recession that began in 2008. President Obama's administration passed it through congress in 2010.

This Dodd-Frank Act legislation is literally thousands of pages long and contains numerous provisions. The regulations of this Dodd-Frank Act law are set for implementation over the course of a number of years. They were meant to reduce the obvious risks for failure in the American financial system. In order to oversee and carry out the numerous parts of the act it addresses, the controversial legislation created a range of new government agencies.

The first of these new agencies is the Financial Stability Oversight Council and Orderly Liquidation Authority. This group is tasked with overseeing major financial firms whose continued financial stability is necessary for the proper and continuous functioning of the U.S. economy.

These companies were negatively referred to as "too big to fail." The agency also handles necessary restructurings or liquidations of such firms in an orderly fashion should they become too unstable. They are charged with preventing these firms from being propped up with tax dollars. This council has great authority. They can even break apart banks which they deem in their judgment to be so big that they pose a risk to the banking system. It may also order higher reserve requirements for such banks. Another new group the Federal Insurance Office is similarly tasked with identifying and overseeing insurance companies which are too important to fail.

The CFPB Consumer Financial Protection Bureau was created to stop predatory forms of mortgage lending by the lenders. They are also responsible for increasing the simplicity of mortgage terms so that consumers can understand what they are signing before they complete the contracts. The group stops mortgage brokers from obtaining larger commissions when they close loans that have higher interest rates and fees.

It states that originators of mortgages may not direct possible borrowers to loans which provide the largest payouts to the loan originators. This group also governs various other kinds of lending to consumers. Their domain includes debt and credit cards and consumer complaints. They insist that lenders provide information in a manner that is simplest for consumers to comprehend. Credit card application simplified terms are an example of their work.

One potent rule that emerged from this Dodd-Frank Act legislation proved to be the so-called Volcker Rule. Named for the former Federal Reserve Chairman Paul Volcker, the rule was intended to reduce the amount of speculative trading, while simultaneously banning proprietary trading, by banking institutions. Banks have complained that these changes in the business model will make it more difficult to stay profitable.

The rule addresses regulating the derivatives like the infamous credit default swaps that majorly contributed to the financial meltdown in 2008. This rule also limits the ability of financial companies to utilize derivatives. The goal is to stop the systemically critical institutions from building up enormous risks that could ruin the banking system and overall economy.

The Dodd-Frank Act further created the new SEC Office of Credit Ratings. This group received the job of watching the credit agencies to ensure that the credit ratings they provide for various entities prove to be both dependable and reliable. Credit rating companies received a lot of blame for the financial crisis for falsely dispensing investment ratings that were misleading and overly positive.

Critics of the Dodd-Frank Act legislation claim the law will hamper economic growth and lead to higher unemployment in the future. Fans of the act insist that over time it will reduce the chances of the economy suffering from another 2008 styled crisis all the while safeguarding consumers from the abuses that eventually led to the crisis.

European Central Bank (ECB)

The European Central Bank is responsible for the European Union's monetary system and for maintaining the euro currency. The EU created this central bank of European central banks in June of 1998. It works alongside the various national banks of the EU member states to come up with unified monetary policy. This policy is intended to help achieve price stability throughout the countries in the EU.

The ECB became responsible for the EU's monetary police on January 1 of 1999. This was the point in time when the euro currency became adopted by the various EU nations. This landmark event was the culmination of 20 years of steps towards a currency union.

In 1979, eight of the EU nations created the EMS European Monetary System. It effectively fixed the exchange rates between the eight participating nations. By 2002, the ECB had become more entrenched. Twelve EU nations signed on to a common monetary policy and formed the European Economic and Monetary Union that year.

The European Central Bank is independent of political groups in the various institutions of the EU such as the European Commission, European Parliament, and European Council. It handles all EU monetary issues and policies. Maintaining price stability is the first goal of the central bank. It also sets the important interest rates for the Eurozone and area.

Besides creating monetary policy for the Eurozone block, the ECB also engages in foreign exchange, holds reserve currencies, and authorizes euro bank note issues. Euro currency is actually created, printed, and maintained by the European System of Central Banks, also known as the ESCB.

The ECB has become involved in some controversial activities which were beyond the scope of its original role. It has further expanded its mandate in recent years by buying up bonds of financial companies like banks and also sovereign countries whose bonds are not finding enough interested subscribers at competitive low rates.

They have been practicing this quantitative easing and injecting money into euro area economies in an effort to encourage growth and to increase financial liquidity in the banking system. Keeping the interest rates down on sovereign national bonds also improves the budgets and balance sheets of the euro area countries which are struggling. The result of these activities has led to negative real interest rates in Europe.

Individual EU countries collect their own taxes. They also determine their own national budgets. The ECB has nothing to do with these activities. National governments work together at the EU level to come up with uniform rules on public finances. This helps them to cooperate better on policies for employment, growth, and financial stability.

The financial crisis that broke out around the globe in 2008 hit some European countries especially hard. It created a need for the ECB to work closely with the European Commission and the national governments of the EU and Eurozone members in a series of coordinated, sustained actions.

These groups are continuing to strive together to promote employment and growth, keep credit flowing to consumers and businesses at affordable prices, safeguard savings, and to guarantee inter-European financial stability. This has led to the accusation of critics of the European institutions that they only work effective when there are crises, as in a management by crisis style.

Despite these ongoing and best efforts of the ECB and other European institutions, severe imbalances and problems remain in several Eurozone countries. As of 2016, unemployment in Spain still sat at over 25% and Greece teetered on the brink of yet another recession and potential insolvency.

European Investment Bank (EIB)

The European Investment Bank proves to be the bank of the European Union. As such it is the one and only bank which is both representing the EU member states' interests and also owned by the same member countries. This EIB works hand in glove with the other institutions of the European Union in order to carry out the common EU policies.

This European Investment Bank turns out to be the biggest multilateral lender and borrower on the planet. It delivers finance via loans and joint ventures as well as expertise to support projects of sustainable investments. While over 90 percent of the bank's projects remain in Europe, they are still a substantially large investor throughout the globe.

The European Investment Bank betters the quality of life for individuals within and without the continent of Europe by offering expertise and finance on projects which encourage SME's (small to medium enterprises), infrastructure, innovation, and climate action. Their enormous and far flung enterprises in areas of lending, blending, and advisory services work for the good of EU residents and citizens, along with residents of numerous countries which are not a part of the European Union.

Lending is the overwhelming center of activity for the European Investment Bank. By far the greatest share of the bank's financing occurs via loans. They do also provide microfinance, guarantees, and equity investment, among other types of financing. The bank is able to harness their vast financial resources in order to borrow money on the world markets at extremely competitive rates. They then deliver these cost savings to those projects which they deem to be economically practical and which foster the objectives of EU policy.

Lending accounts for nearly 90 percent of all their financial commitments. The European Investment Bank actually lends money to clients of all sizes and purposes in order to encourage jobs and sustainable growth. The support of this well-regarded institution tends to attract other investors to the projects. Such projects must be over 25 million Euros in order to qualify for a loan. They also facilitate intermediated loans through local area banks.

With their venture capital program, they assist fund managers to invest capital in growth area SME's and high technology companies. Microfinance they offer for both fund and equity investments as well.

Blending is the tool whereby the European Investment Bank helps to release funding from other financial sources by collaborating on a project. This support especially comes out of the EU budget. When blended along with loans, it helps to ensure a fully financed package of investment in a given project.

The EIB offers structured finance to give support to high priority projects. Guarantees ensure that a good project will be able to bring in sufficient new investment from other partners. Project bonds help to unlock funding for infrastructure projects. The InnovFin initiative delivers innovators EU based finance. The bank also partners with donors in trust funds. They support transport infrastructure and the JEREMIE project which delivers financial engineering and flexible finance to SME enterprises.

Other blending programs include ESIF Financial Instruments, the JESSICA program which supports urban development, the Private Finance for Energy Efficiency (PF4EE) program, and the Mutual Reliance Initiative offering efficient partnerships for development and growth.
Blending programs also include the Natural Capital Financing Facility to combine the bank's financing with that of the European Commission as part of the LIFE Program to assist climate and environmental actions. An interesting last blending program proves to be the Risk Capital Facility for the Southern Neighborhood. This gives access to debt and equity financing for SMEs found throughout the Mediterranean regions. Its goal is to foster growth which is inclusive, job creation in the private sector, and development in the private sector.

Advising services provide technical assistance and expertise in the form of project and administrative management capabilities. This helps to bring in other investment. Both pubic authorities and private companies are able to rely on the technical and financial experience of the European Investment Advisory Hub to make sure the entity obtains the best people needed for a given project.

European Monetary System (EMS)

In 1979 a few European nations linked their currencies together in an arrangement and system to stabilize exchange rates called the European Monetary System. This system endured until the EMU European Economic and Monetary Union succeeded it.

As an important institution within the European Union, the EMU established the euro. The origin of the EMS lay in an effort to reduce significant changes in exchange rates between the European nations and to reign in inflation. It led to the creation of the European Central Bank in June of 1998 and the euro in January of 1999.

After the failure of the defunct Bretton Woods Agreement in 1972, the Europeans wanted to create a new exchange rate system of their own to help encourage political and economic unity throughout the EU. They came up with the EMS in 1979 as a means of moving towards the common currency of the future.

The EMS eventually formed its successor the European Currency Unit. With the ECU, exchange rates could be formulated by methods that were official. In the first year of the EMS, currency values proved to be uneven. Adjustments had to be made to lower weaker currencies while increasing the stronger currency values. In 1986 they came up with a more stable system of altering national interest rates instead.

Crisis broke out in the EMS in the early years of the 1990s. Germany's reunification created political and economic conditions that made the exchange rate bands less workable. Britain withdrew permanently from EMS in 1992. They became more independent from the central EU this way and banded together with Denmark and Sweden in refusing to become members of the eurozone.

This did not stop other nations within the EU from continuing to push for closer economic integration and a common currency. They formed the European Monetary Institute in 1994 to set up an orderly transition to the ECB that arose in 1998. The main tasks of the new ECB were to come up with one interest rate and monetary policy by laboring alongside the national central banks.

The ECB was not given the role originally of lending money to governments in financial crises or increasing employment rates like the majority of central banks. This would later cause delays and problems in bailing out struggling countries in the financial crisis that began in earnest in 2008.

The end of 1998 saw the majority of nations in the EU cut their interest rates at the same time to encourage economic growth while preparing to implement the Euro currency. This is when they established the EMU to succeed the EMS as the primary economic policy mechanism in the European Union. The adoption and subsequent circulation of the euro by the eurozone countries proved to be a significant step towards the aimed for European political unity. The EMU has helped member nations attempt to work toward lower inflation, less public spending, and lesser government debts.

Hidden weaknesses in the European Monetary System became obvious during the global financial crisis of 2008 and the following years. Member nations like Greece, Portugal, Spain, Ireland, and Cyprus ran up high deficits that later erupted in the European sovereign debt crisis.

Because these countries did not have national currencies to devalue, they could not increase their exports. The EMU forbade them from spending additional money and running higher deficits to help increase employment. EMS policies had expressly forbidden eurozone bailouts to any countries whose economies were in trouble.

After months of arguments from the larger economy members such as Germany and France, the EMU at last came up with bailout policies that allowed aid to be dispensed to peripheral members who were struggling. They set up the European Stability Mechanism as a permanent pool of money to help out economies of struggling EU member states in 2012. This allowed a few of the countries in trouble like Spain, Portugal, and Ireland to make some progress on recoveries.

European Stability Mechanism (ESM)

The European Stability Mechanism is a significant part of the financial stability and safeguard mechanisms in the Euro Zone area. It replaced the EFSF European Financial Stability Facility in 2013. This original EFSF was never intended to be permanent. Instead it was designed as a temporary solution to financial problems within the EU.

The European Stability Mechanism that took over for it was better established to deliver financial help to those Eurozone member countries that found themselves either threatened by or actually experiencing financial difficulties.

These two financial facilities ran concurrently from October of 2012 through June of 2013. Beginning in July of 2013 the EFSF could no longer begin new programs for financial support or help. The program still exists to manage and collect repayments of debts that are outstanding.

Once all of the existing loans that the EFSF program made have been repaid and all funding instruments and guarantors have received full payment for their contributions, then the EFSF will cease to exist entirely. This makes the replacing ESM the only and ongoing internal means for delivering aid in response to new calls for financial assistance from Eurozone member nations.

The European Stability Mechanism proves to be the principal means of resolving crises for nations which participate in the Euro. It obtains its money by issuing debt obligations. This permits it to fund financial aid and loans to the member countries of the Euro area. The European Council actually created the ESM in December of 2010. Participating Euro member states came together and signed a treaty between the governments on February 2 of 2012. October 8 of 2012 was the day they inaugurated the new ESM.

This ESM has great flexibility in funding its distressed member states. As various conditions are met, it is able to deliver loans as part of a program for macroeconomic adjustment. The mechanism is also able to buy member countries' debt in either the secondary or primary markets.

It can help to recapitalize banks of member states by loaning the governments money for this purpose. It can also deliver credit lines as a means of providing financial help as a precaution. In worst case and last resort conditions, the facility is allowed to recapitalize banks and other financial institutions directly. This is limited to times when resolution funds and bail ins are not enough to make the bank financially viable again.

The resources of the ESM are considerable. It has a capital base that has been subscribed in the amount of 704.8 billion. Of this amount, 80.5 billion has been paid in to the facility. The remaining 624.3 billion is classified as callable capital when it is needed. The fund is able to loan out a maximum total of 500 billion.

The ESM is based in Luxembourg. It is governed by public international law as an intergovernmental organization. It has only government shareholders making up its ownership. These are the 19 member countries that make up the Euro area. In 2016, 153 staff members worked under the direction of Klaus Regling the managing director.

European countries which are in trouble have other outside recourses for help besides the ESM. The principal other provider of assistance is the International Monetary Fund. The EU has supported having its own ESM, along with the predecessors the EFSF and the European Financial Stabilization Mechanism because it feared the consequences of some of its member states' problems with debt. Not all of the EZ countries suffered from debt issues. One EZ country failing could have contagious effects and widespread repercussions on the other national economies' health.

Fannie Mae

Fannie Mae is the acronym for the FNMA Federal National Mortgage Association. This entity is a GSE Government Sponsored Enterprise along with brother organization Freddie Mac. It became a publicly traded company in 1968. This home lending giant proves to be the largest mortgage financing provider anywhere in the United States. As such, it funds significantly more mortgages than any competing company or entity. It ensures that homebuyers, homeowners, and renters around the U.S. all can obtain financing options which they can afford.

As the GSE became established in 1938, it has provided funding for the housing market of the country for over 75 years. Franklin D. Roosevelt's New Deal established the company in the midst of the Great Depression. This is why the mission of the company is to aid individuals in purchasing, renting, or refinancing a home whether economic times in the country are good or bad.

The company's explicit purpose is to boost the size of the secondary mortgage market. They do this when they securitize mortgages and package them into MBS mortgage backed securities. This process returns the mortgage loaned money to lenders who are then able to reinvest this money into additional lending. It also acts to grow the numbers of lending institutions who are issuing mortgages. This ensures that there are more than just savings and loan associations making local loans for housing.

The model worked well until between 2003 and 2004. At this point the subprime mortgages crisis started. It began when the mortgage market turned away from the GSEs like Freddie Mac and Fannie Mae and began to migrate rapidly to unregulated MBS Mortgage Backed Securities that major investment banks put together. This shift to private MBSs caused the GSEs to lose their control over and ability to monitor mortgages in the country.

Increased competition between the investment banks and the GSEs reduced the power and market share of the government mortgage backers further and boosted the mortgage lenders at their expense. This radical change in the way mortgages were overseen and made caused the underwriting standards for mortgages to dangerously decline. It turned out to be one of the major reasons for the ensuing mortgage and financial crises.

The situation became so severe at Fannie Mae by 2008 that the FHFA Federal Housing Finance Agency had to get directly involved. FHFA Director James Lockhart on September 7, 2008 placed both this organization and Freddie Mac under FHFA conservatorship. This proved to be among the most dramatic and far reaching government involvements in free enterprise financial markets for literally decades.

Among Lockhart's first actions, he fired both companies' boards of directors and CEOs. He then made the companies issue a new class of common stock warrants and senior preferred stock to Treasury for 79.9% of both GSEs. Those who had been holding either preferred or common stock in either entity before the conservatorship began saw the value of their shares massively decrease. All prior shares' dividends became suspended to try to hold up the mortgage backed securities' and company debt values. FHFA pledged that it had no intentions of liquidating the GSEs.

Since 2009, Fannie Mae has made great strides in its business of helping make housing work better for individuals and families. They have injected trillions of dollars into the mortgage markets in lending liquidity. This has gone a long way to helping the housing markets and overall economy to recover.

The company has also gone back to high quality eligibility and underwriting standards. In the first quarter of 2016, they have extended $115 billion in mortgage credit that has allowed for 210,000 homes to be purchased and 256,000 mortgages to be refinanced. They also financed the construction of 161,000 multifamily rental units.

Federal Deposit Insurance Corporation (FDIC)

The U.S. government started The Federal Deposit Insurance Corporation back in 1933. They created it because of the literally thousands of failed banks that went down in the 1920s and 1930s. The FDIC began insuring bank accounts at the beginning of 1934. Since then, no depositors have lost any insured bank account money despite a consistent number of banks failing every year.

The first role of the FDIC is to insure and to increase the public's confidence in the American banking system. They do this in several ways. The FDIC insures minimally $250,000 in bank and thrift accounts. They watch for and take action on any risks to the deposit insurance funds. They also stop the spread of any bank failures when one of the banks does fail.

The Federal Deposit Insurance Corporation only insures deposits. This means that it does not cover mutual funds, stocks, or any other investments that some banks offer to their customers. They offer a standard $250,000 amount for each depositor's account. This single limit amount does not apply to other types of account ownerships and accounts at other banks. To help individuals understand if the insurance provided is enough to cover their various kinds of account, the FDIC provides its Electronic Deposit Insurance Estimator.

Another important role of the FDIC lies in its supervisory position. The outfit oversees over 4,500 different savings and commercial banks to make sure that they are operationally safe and sound. This represents more than half of the banks. Those banks that are set up as state banks may choose to become a member of either the Federal Reserve System or the FDIC. Any banks that are not overseen by the Federal Reserve System are watched over by the FDIC.

Another job of the FDIC is to check on the various banks to make sure they abide by the government's consumer protection laws. These laws include The Fair Credit Reporting Act, the Fair Credit Billing Act, the Fair Debt Collection Practices Act, and the Truth in Lending Act.

Lastly, the FDIC checks banks to make sure the different institutions are abiding by their responsibilities under the Community Reinvestment Act.

This law ensures that banks help the communities where they were started to achieve their needs for credit.

Despite all of these roles, the only one that members of the public really encounter on a personal basis is the FDIC protecting insured depositors. When a bank or thrift goes down, the FDIC immediately reacts to the situation. They come in fast with the group that chartered the bank to close it down. The charter group could be the Office of the Comptroller of the Currency or the state regulator.

The next step is for the FDIC to wind up the failed bank. In their preferred method, they sell both the loans and the deposits of the bank to another banking institution. Customers rarely feel the transition in the majority of the cases. This is the FDIC's goal, to make sure that people do not lose access to their accounts and money.

The FDIC carries out its several mandates through six regional branches. It has more than 7,000 staff members that help it to carry out these goals. The organization is based in its headquarters in the capital Washington, D.C. Besides these locations, they also have various field offices throughout the nation.

The leadership of the FDIC is supplied by the Federal Government. The President appoints the board which the Senate confirms. There are five members of their Board of Directors. No more than three of them may belong to one political party to ensure bipartisanship in the decisions.

Federal Reserve

The Federal Reserve, also known as the Fed, or the Federal Reserve Board, proves to be the United States' central banking system. This central bank came about in 1913 as a result of Congress passing the Federal Reserve Act. Congress created the organization because of a number of serious financial panics that culminated in the severe panic of 1907.

With time, the Federal Reserve's roles and areas of responsibility have grown as the organization has expanded. Economic events such as the Great Depression have only served to encourage this.

The Federal Reserve today counts among its duties many responsibilities. Among these are regulating and overseeing the country's banks, managing the country's monetary policy and supply, assuring the financial systems' continuance and stability, and offering a variety of financial services to depositing banks, foreign central banks, and the United States government.

The Federal Reserve's structure is made up of a number of different components. Among these are the Federal Reserve Board of Governors, all of whom are appointed by the President. The Federal Open Market Committee, also known by its acronym of FOMC, sets the monetary policy, like the interest rates, for the nation. There are also Federal Reserve Banks, which are twelve regional institutions that are found in the biggest area cities around America. They offer physical currency to member banks when demand proves to be unusually high. Several councils that advise it are a part of The Federal Reserve, as are technically the member banks throughout the country.

The FOMC component of the Federal Reserve is actually comprised of all of these seven Board of Governors members along with the presidents of the twelve regional banks. Only five of these presidents are voting members at a time. Together, they review the state of the U.S. national economy in order to determine what fiscal policies need to be pursued. When the economic growth is slowing, or a recession is occurring, they cut the national interest rates. When inflation is appearing or the economy is overheating, they raise these interest rates.

The Federal Reserve proves to be a unique entity among the major central banks. This is because it divides up the various responsibilities into some public and some private parts of the institution. The Federal Reserve furthermore serves to create the currency used for the country, the U.S. dollar. The fact that it is both a public and private institution, with so many varied and vast powers, makes it one of a kind.

Because the U.S. dollar is still the reserve currency of the world, the Federal Reserve's powers are far greater than simply managing the U.S. economy. In actual practice, they also are the custodians and managers of the world's reserve currency. This gives them considerable power and influence throughout the entire world economy, since they are able to create not only dollars for the U.S. economy, but also for other central banks use in foreign countries. As a result of this, more than half of the physically printed U.S. dollars are found outside of the United States.

Federal Reserve Act of 1913

The Federal Reserve Act of 1913 created the Federal Reserve Bank. This proved to be the Act of Congress that set up the Federal Reserve System. This system became the Central Bank organization for the United States. As part of the act, the Federal Reserve acquired the powers to issue the nation's legal tender currency. President Woodrow Wilson actually signed this act, making it law in 1913.

The leadership of the country felt the need to create such a central bank for several reasons. The United States had operated without a central bank going back to the expiration of the Second Bank of the United States' charter. This meant that for about eighty years, the country had existed without any form of central bank.

In time, a number of financial panics had ensued without any central bank to intervene in them. The one that really galvanized congressional and public opinion for having a central bank proved to be the serious financial panic of 1907. As a result of these factors, a number of Americans decided that the nation required serious currency and banking reforms that could handle such panics by offering an available liquid assets' reserve. They also figured such an institution might be capable of managing a consistent expansion and contraction of credit and currency from time to time as appropriate.

The original Federal Reserve Act plan recommended an establishment of an unusual combined public and private entity system. They suggested that minimally eight and as many as twelve regional private Federal Reserve banks should be created. All of them were to have their own boards of directors, regional boundary lines, and branches. This new entity would be led by a Federal Reserve Board comprised of seven members and made up of public officials that the President appointed and the Senate would confirm. An advisory committee known as the Federal Advisory Committee would be created, along with a brand new U.S. currency that would alone be accepted nationally, the Federal Reserve Note. In the final version of the bill, twelve regional Federal Reserve Banks were actually created. The rest of the above provisions became law and subsequently a part of the newly created Federal Reserve System.

Another important decision that Congress settled on with the Federal Reserve Act revolved around the private banks throughout the U.S. Every nationally chartered bank had to join the Federal Reserve System as a part of this act. They were made to buy stock that could not be transferred in their own area's Federal Reserve Bank. It furthermore required that a set dollar total of reserves that did not pay interest had to be deposited to their own regional Federal Reserve Bank. Banks that are only state chartered have the choice, but not the obligation, of joining this system and being regulated by the Fed.

Finally, the act allowed the member banks to receive loans at a discounted rate from the discount windows of their own regional Federal Reserve Bank. They were promised a six percent yearly dividend on their Federal Reserve stock and provided with additional services. The act also gave the Federal Reserve Banks the authority to assume the role of U.S. government fiscal agents.

Federal Reserve Bank

Twelve different Federal Reserve Banks make up the Federal Reserve System that functions as the central bank for the U.S. Federal reserve banks are also utilized to sub-divide up the country into the twelve Federal Reserve Districts.

Every Federal Reserve Bank bears the responsibility for individually regulating the various commercial banks that are found in such a bank's geographical district. Ensuring the continuation of the financial system and all of the member banks is among the primary responsibilities of the Federal Reserve System.

Each Federal Reserve Bank also issues its own stock shares that can only be acquired by participating member banks. The banks are required to obtain these shares by law. While the shares may not be traded, pledged as a loan security, or sold, they do pay dividends that run as high as six percent each year.

American banks are required by law to keep certain fractional reserves of their actual deposits. These are mostly held by the regional Federal Reserve Banks. Although in years past, the Federal Reserve did not pay member banks interest on these funds kept on reserve, as of 2008 Congress passed the EESA that permits them to pay the participating banks interest.

The twelve Federal Reserve Banks and districts are found geographically spread out around the nation. They include the Federal Reserve Banks of Boston, New York, Philadelphia, Cleveland, Richmond, Atlanta, Chicago, St. Louis, Minneapolis, Kansas City, Dallas, and San Francisco.

The largest and still most important of the individual Federal Reserve Banks proves to be the Federal Reserve Bank of New York. Not only does this bank have the greatest asset base of all the twelve branches, valued at over a trillion dollars and representing four times the asset base of the next largest Federal Reserve Bank, but it also boasts the biggest gold depository on earth, valued at in excess of $25 billion. The gold kept in the New York Federal Reserve Bank vaults belongs to other nations who store it there for safe keeping. Saudi Arabia and Kuwait both keep their significant holdings here.

Among the various states that have Federal Reserve Banks headquartered there, a few of them contain more than one branch within their state. California, Missouri, and Tennessee are the ones that make this claim. Tennessee actually contains two branches from two different districts within its state boundaries. The only state that has two Federal Reserve Banks headquartered within it is Missouri. For the largest geographical areas covered by the districts, San Francisco is the largest, Kansas City is second biggest, and Minneapolis is the third largest.

Fractional Banking System

The fractional banking system is also known as the fractional reserve banking system. This system is the way that virtually all modern day banks around the world operate. In a fractional reserve banking system, banks actually only maintain a small amount of their deposited funds in reserve forms of cash and other easily liquid assets.

The rest of the deposits they loan out, even though all of their deposits are allowed to be withdrawn at the customers' demand. Fractional banking happens any time that banks loan out money that they bring in from deposits.

Fractional banking systems are ones where banks constantly expand the money supply beyond the levels at which they exist. Because of this, total money supplies are commonly a multiple bigger than simply the currency created by the nation's central bank. The multiple is also known as the money multiplier. Its amount is determined by a reserve requirement that the financial overseers set.

This fractional reserve system is managed ultimately by central banks and these reserve requirements that they enforce. On the one hand, it sets a limit on the quantity of money that is created by the commercial banks. The other purpose of it is to make certain that banks keep enough readily available cash in order to keep up with typical withdrawal demands of customers. Even though this is the case, there can be problems. Should many depositors at once attempt to take out their money, then a run on the bank might occur. If this happens on a large national or regional scale, the possibility of a banking systemic crisis emerges.

Central banks attempt to reduce these problems. They keep a close eye on commercial banks through regulations and oversight. Besides that, they promise to help out banks that fall into difficulties by acting as their ultimate lender of last resort. Finally, central banks instill confidence in the fractional reserve banking system by guaranteeing the deposits of the customers of the commercial banks.

A significant amount of criticism has been leveled against this fractional reserve banking system. Mainstream critics have complained that because money is only created as individuals borrow from the banking system, the system itself forces people to take on debt in order for money to actually be created. They say that this debases the currency. The biggest problem that they have with the commercial banking system growing the money supply is that it is literally creating money from nothing.

Other critics associate fractional banking with fiat currencies, or money that is only valuable because the governments say that they are. They decry these as negative aspects of current money systems. They dislike that fractional banking systems and fiat money together do not place any limits on how much a money supply can ultimately grow. This can lead to bubbles in both capital markets and assets, such as real estate, stock markets, and commodities. All of these can be victims of speculation, which is made easier by the creation of money through debt in the fractional reserve system.

Freddie Mac

Freddie Mac is a semi-private company that Congress chartered in 1970. They created the entity to offer stability, liquidity, and affordable prices for the country and its housing markets. They have grown to be responsible for the home purchases of one out of four buyers.

Besides this the company is also among the biggest financing sources for multifamily housing in the nation. From 2009 to 2016, the company has dispersed mortgage market funding that amounts to over $2.5 trillion. This has enabled in excess of 13 million American families to refinance, purchase, or rent a home in that time frame.

In 1970 Congress was seeking to stabilize the mortgage markets of the country. They wanted to grow and improve opportunities for rental housing that was affordable and for home buying. Because of this, Freddie Mac's mission has always been to bring stability, liquidity, and affordability to the national housing market in the United States. They do this in a variety of ways. The company helps the secondary mortgage market. They buy both mortgage securities and mortgage loans outright as investments. They then package and sell these as guaranteed mortgage securities known as PCs. In this secondary market, there are entities which buy and sell mortgages as complete loans or as mortgage securities. Freddie Mac never makes loans to home owners directly themselves.

Because of the collapse of the mortgage backed securities markets in 2007 and 2008 and its impact on their finances, the company is now being run under conservatorship. The FHFA Federal Housing Finance Agency oversees their business to make sure loans are carefully scrutinized and securitized. They want to avoid the mistakes of the financial crisis becoming repeated here.

Freddie Mac operates in three main business areas to ensure that a continuous supply of mortgage funding goes through to the housing markets in the country. They make rental housing and home buying more affordable through their single family credit guarantee business, their multifamily business, and their investment business. They utilize all three of these to promote financing for affordable housing.

The single family line is essentially a recycling operation. They work with securitizing mortgages so that the entity is able to provide funding to millions of different home loans annually. This securitization proves to be the means where they buy up different loans lenders have made and then package these up into various mortgage securities. They then sell these on the worldwide capital markets. The money from the sale of these securities they next funnel back to the lenders. In this way home loan operations have sufficient mortgage money for lending.

The company is also interested in supporting renters as well. This is the role of their multifamily business. In this line, the outfit cooperates with a group of lenders to help finance the construction of various apartment buildings throughout the United States. The lenders make the loans and Freddie Mac buys them to package and resell. This way the lenders receive back the proceeds so they can issue more loans. This is a critical line as multifamily loans prove to be a few million dollars each and require unique underwriting from one property to the next.

Their investment business actually purchases some of their own mortgage backed securities which they and other financial entities like Fannie Mae guarantee. This portfolio further invests into individual loans which they guarantee but choose not to securitize. By bidding on some of their own securities, the investment business and portfolio serves the markets. It gives these mortgage backed securities greater liquidity and offers more funding for mortgages. They do this by issuing their own debt which creates net income for the company after they pay their interest to the bond holders.

Glass Steagall Act

Congress created and passed the Glass Steagall Act in 1933. This legislation arose because of the effects of the 1929 catastrophic stock market crash. Two congressmen came up with this solution in the Great Depression when many banks were failing. The law made separate all activities which involved commercial banking and investment banking.

Commercial banks had become heavily involved in the stock market. This activity received much of the blame for the stock market and financial crashes. Lawmakers felt that commercial banks had employed money from their depositors in speculation in the stock market.

The reasons this act came forcefully into law had to do with banks' activities. Commercial banks had bought new and unproven stocks to sell to individual customers. It was the greed of banks that led to the new legislation. The goals of banking were mired in conflict of interest. Banks would make loans to corporations in which they already had an investment. These loans were not issued based on good underwriting.

They would then push these investments to their clients. Their goal was to have their customers help support these companies. Such commercial speculation insured that when the companies failed, the banks and their customers all lost huge amounts of money. Finally banks began to collapse in the thousands as a result of this poor and unregulated activity.

The act actually came about because of Senator Carter Glass. Glass had served as Treasury secretary previously. He also founded the U.S. Federal Reserve System. The failing banks motivated him to act on a bill. He became the main driving force of this legislation. His partner on the project was Henry Bascom Stegall.

Stegall served as House Banking and Currency Committee chairman. At first he would not support the bill with Glass. They added an amendment to create insurance for bank deposits. This brought Congressman Steagall's critical support of the act.

The effects of this Glass Steagall Act erected a variety of barriers in the banking industry. A new firewall of regulation arose between investment bank and commercial bank businesses. The two types of banks experienced unprecedented oversight and control over their activities. All banks received one year to choose a specialty in either investment banking or commercial banking.

Those that chose commercial banking were heavily limited in their investment banking activities. Income from securities could not exceed 10% of the commercial bank earnings. Commercial banks were permitted to underwrite bonds the government issued. The ultimate goal was to stop banks from committing their depositors' funds to projects which were poorly underwritten and speculative.

Banks that were too big to fail at the time became significant targets for this act. JP Morgan and Company and rival financial empires were among these. Such outfits had to eliminate many services. This targeted a large and important part of their incomes.

Later on criticism of the Glass Steagall Act arose. This happened as different explanations became popular for the Great Depression. Many different individuals also saw that this act had created problems for financial services. They blamed the law for restricting financial firms to the point that they were not able to compete effectively.

Many opposed the act by the 1980s. Glass Steagall opposition grew into the 1990s. Congress finally repealed the act in 1999. The elimination of this act has been blamed for the Great Recession crisis that started in 2006.

Banks were again able to mix investment and lending activities. Close regulation of commercial banks had been largely eliminated. Because of this, banks again made many risky loans that were either liar loans or not properly documented for income.

Gold Standard

The gold standard represents a centuries' used system of money for backing up currencies with tangible, physical gold holdings in a central bank vault. Under the gold standard, the basic economic currency unit proved to be a pre set amount of gold by weight. Several different types of gold standards exist.

The Gold specie standard proves to be a system where the money unit itself is represented by gold coins that are in circulation. Alternatively, it could be represented by an exchange unit of value that is literally expressed in units against a specific gold coin that circulates, along with other coins that are minted from a metal with less value, such as silver or copper.

Conversely, the gold exchange standard usually has to do with silver and other valuable metal coins that are circulating. In this type of exchange system, the monetary authorities promise that a set exchange rate against the currency of another country practicing the gold standard will be maintained. This gives rise to a gold standard that is not literal but still de facto. The silver coins circulating then trade with a set external value in gold terms that stands independently of the actual silver value contained within the coins.

The most common gold standard that has been seen in the last few hundred years turns out to be the gold bullion standard. The gold bullion standard refers to a money system where no gold coins are actually circulating throughout the economy. Instead, the monetary authorities have consented to exchange a set amount of gold in exchange for their paper currency. This is done at a set price that is established for the paper currency that circulates.

The gold bullion standard existed in the world economy from the 1700's until 1971. During this span of almost three hundred years, the values of major world currencies proved to be exceptionally stable, as were the supplies of money in existence. This resulted from a restriction of the gold standard that only allowed such paper currency to be printed as greater amounts of gold existed in the respective nation's treasury and vaults. The positive of this proved to be that the world could count on currencies that did not fluctuate wildly in value or decline consistently over time. Governments disliked the gold standard as it kept them from increasing the money supply or spending more money than the country actually had. They found it too restrictive.

The gold standard in the world collapsed when President Nixon initiated what became known as the Nixon shock by unilaterally taking the country off of gold exchange and convertibility for dollars in 1971. The currency of both the U.S. and most countries of the world then became Fiat currencies, only backed up by the government decree. Since the gold standard was abandoned, the U.S. dollar has declined so severely that a single dollar in 1971 would today be worth $35 2010 dollars.

Goldman Sachs

Goldman Sachs is an American based investment bank. The global company proves to be among the largest and most successful securities, investment banking, and investment management firms. It delivers an extensive variety of financial services to a client base that is diverse and significant. Among its clientele are financial institutions, corporations, individuals, and governments.

The group was founded in 1869. Its headquarters remain in New York City. Goldman Sachs' keeps offices in all of the important worldwide financial centers. Their office network spans over 35 countries and employs almost 35,000 staff. For 2015, the company boasted profits of $8.77 billion on revenues amounting to $39.2 billion. Goldman operates in four groups which include Investment Banking, Institutional Client Services, Investing and Lending, and Investment Management.

With the Investment Banking group, Goldman Sachs offers an impressive array of services for investment banking to a varied client base of financial institutions, corporations, governments, and investment funds. These services cover a broad range of needs. Among them are equity and debt underwriting for private placements and public offerings.

The firm also provides strategic advice for divestures, mergers and acquisitions, restructurings, corporate defense activities, risk management, and spin offs. They offer international and local financing of acquisitions and transactions along with relevant derivative transactions. In the year 2015, this group earned revenues of $7 billion.

The Institutional Client Services division works with the group's large institutional clients. They make markets for a number of investments such as equity, fixed income, commodities, and currency pairs on behalf of these clients which include governments, investment funds, corporations, and financial institutions. The group clears transactions for clients via important futures, options, and stock market exchanges around the world. They deliver prime brokerage services, securities lending, and financing for these customers as well. This segment showed revenues of $15.2 billion for 2015, making it twice as large as the next biggest group.

The Investing and Lending operations finance their clients. This includes both originating loans and investing in them. This longer term loan and investment operation covers private and public equity securities, real estate, and loans and debt securities. They make these both directly and indirectly through outside funds. For year 2015, the segment earned $5.4 billion in revenues.

Investment Management operations delivers investment products and services mostly via commingled and separately managed accounts. This includes private investments and mutual funds in all of the important asset classes. They offer these services to both wealthy individual and institutional clients. They also provide high net worth families and individuals with advisory services for their wealth. This includes financial counseling, portfolio management, and brokerage transaction services. In 2015, this segment earned $6.2 billion.

Goldman Sachs suffered dramatically from the 2008 financial crisis because of its heavy involvement with subprime mortgages. The U.S. government had to rescue the group to keep it from failing. They had to convert to a traditional bank with Federal Reserve oversight. Since then, it has massively returned to profitability and repaid its loans.

There are numerous important alumnus among the one time Goldman Sachs executives. These include former Treasury Secretaries like Henry Paulson and Robert Rubin, current European Central Bank President Mario Draghi, and Mark Carney the current Governor of the Bank of England.

Hank Paulson

Hank Paulson is the nickname for Henry M Paulson, Jr. who served as Secretary of the Treasury from 2006 to 2009. Paulson came to Treasury well prepared for the almost unprecedented economic challenges he would face when he arrived in July of 2006. Before becoming secretary, he worked in finance for 32 years with Goldman Sachs, a leading American based global investment bank. While at Goldman, he served as CEO and Chairman of the Board for eight years.

One of Hank Paulson's first endeavors at Treasury was to bring together a diverse group of well experienced professionals so that he could restart the once routine meetings for the President's Working Group on Financial Markets. These strenuous efforts from the financial regulators of the President's Working Group subsequently proved to be key for the efforts of the American government to stave off the complete collapse of the U.S. and global financial systems.

Paulson demonstrated a rare non partisan form of leadership in the critical moments of the crisis. He persuaded Congress to provide him with the historically unparalleled emergency powers which he required to stop the crisis. The man headed the economic team for President George W. Bush with creating and coordinating an impressive and ultimately successful international and national strategy to the 2008 crisis.

This Financial Crisis and Great Recession proved to be the worst the country and globe had seen since the 1930's era Great Depression. Thanks to his decisive actions and courage to face the challenges, he helped to keep the U.S. financial system from collapsing. The catastrophe that these efforts avoided could have sent unemployment to levels not known since the 1930s.

Secretary Hank Paulson did not stop with averting the collapse. He and his Treasury colleagues began to come up with a new regulatory frame work to overhaul the outdated financial regulatory structure. Among these much needed reforms were many of the ideas that eventually made it into the Dodd Frank Bill of financial reform legislation which President Obama finally signed into law.

Secretary Paulson is also remembered for having worked with President Bush to see the G20 elevated to the most important global forum for economic recovery and financial reform. He shepherded the first Summit and its work which laid out a blueprint for the future meetings and importance of the group.

Paulson also earned his place in history for changing the way that the United States engages with China. He did this by starting and leading the Strategic Economic Dialogue. These Cabinet level discussions helped to prioritize and address a significant range of economic topics. Paulson's leadership of this group significantly improved the American relationship with China. It produced substantial results ranging from an important ten year framework to coordinate environmental and energy initiatives, to better product safety for trade, to more appropriate flexibility in the range of China's currency. The SED has been continued by the administration of President Obama as the model for ongoing discussions with China.

Secretary Hank Paulson demonstrated his commitment to open investment and free international trade as well. He served a important role regarding a few foreign policy initiatives. This included advancing Free Trade Agreements with Panama, Columbia, South Korea, and Peru.

His efforts to reform the review process for national security helped to foster more foreign investment within the U.S. Paulson's Treasury also worked tirelessly to stop financing of worldwide terrorist organizations. He helped the President to push nonproliferation of nuclear materials. Among his reforms to Treasury were modernizing the department in areas pertaining to Treasury bond issuing and leadership of the environment.

HSBC

HSBC stands for Hong Kong Shanghai Banking Corporation. This largest international bank in the world by balance sheet has over $1.63 trillion in total assets. The British London based banking giant counts more than 47 million customers as part of its international network spanning 71 countries and territories and 6,000 offices around the globe.

HSBC was founded by a British businessman in 1865 to finance the growing trade between the West and Asia, and especially China. Today HSBC remains among the largest and most impressive banking and financial services conglomerate groups in the world by any relevant measure. Their stated goal is to be recognized as the globe's foremost and best respected international bank.

HSBC is operated globally through four major divisions. These include its Commercial Banking, Global Banking and Markets, Private Banking, and Retail Banking and Wealth Management divisions. Among the banking group's many achievements over the centuries, the group was responsible for setting up the modern day Chinese currency and banking system back during the reign of the last Chinese imperial dynasty. This financial and currency system which HSBC established for China is still used today.

HSBC Commercial Banking operates throughout 55 different nations and territories. Their operation covers both developing and developed world markets that are most important to their many customers. The division serves a great variety of customer types, ranging from major multinational corporations to small outfits to medium sized companies. It offers them the financial tools they need to run their operations effectively.

One of the bank's most appealing features is that it can call upon its vast and multinational financial strength to support clients with term loans, project and acquisition finance, and daily working capital. The bank also offers its customers the financial and legal know how to assist them in engaging in effective stock and bond issues and offerings.

The commercial banking group supports specialist staff in four primary fields. Global Liquidity and Cash Management provides businesses with tools to effectively manage their liquidity. The online platform helps the customers to transact payments seamlessly between currencies and countries. Global Trade and Receivable Finance offers financing to suppliers and buyers in the trade cycle so that they can cover their supply chains.

Global Banking offers its commercial customers a variety of services such as capital financing via equity, debt, and advisory services. Insurance and Investments provides protection in the form of financial, business, and trade insurance. It also offers wealth management for corporations, employee benefits, and other commercial insurance products to protect against risk.

The Global Banking and Markets division works with customers to help them access commercial opportunities for developed and developing markets. This division operates in three groups including the corporate sector group, the resources and energy group, and the financial institutions group. Services and products are comprised of financing, advisory, research and analysis, prime services, trading and sales, securities services, and transaction banking.

HSBC Private Bank delivers global private banking services that include wealth management, investment, and private banking services to its individual, business, and executive clients. The division's goal is to become the world's foremost private bank for business owners who are high net worth individuals leveraging the group's longstanding globally leading commercial services and heritage.

Retail Banking and Wealth Management provides its tens of millions of customers with a broad range of products and services. These include personal banking, internet banking, loans, mortgages, savings, insurance, investments, and credit cards. They offer a variety of proprietary services and accounts that include HSBC Premier, HSBC Advance, personal online banking, financial planning, and wealth solutions.

International Bank Account Number (IBAN)

IBAN is an acronym which stands for the International Bank Account Number. This standardized numbering system for identifying bank accounts around the world with precision was first conceived of and implemented by the banks of Europe. They wanted to make simpler the means of transacting between bank accounts of financial institutions based in different countries.

This internationally agreed to system for identifying the world's banks and bank accounts was critically needed for banking across international borders. European banks found it necessary to come up with a way to effectively process the cross border transactions. They wanted to dramatically lower the dangers of errors in transcription and subsequent transmission problems which sometimes resulted.

It was the ECBS European Committee for Banking Standards that first adopted the IBAN concept. It later evolved into a global standard under the auspices of ISO 13616:1997. This standard became updated with ISO directive 13616:2007 that now utilizes SWIFT as the official registrar. The system originally arose as a means of facilitating payments made throughout the European Union. It has now been put into place by the majority of European nations along with many countries throughout the globe, especially in the states of the Caribbean and Middle East. Sixty-nine different nations utilized the IBAN account numbering system as of February 2016. More sign up all the time.

The IBAN account number is made up of several components. The two letter national code comes first. This is followed up by the two check digits which enable an integrity check of the IBAN number to be sure it is correct. Finally come as many as thirty alphanumeric characters which are also called the BBAN, or Basic Bank Account Number. Each national banking association decides which BBAN will become the standard for their own national bank accounts. In general, the remaining thirty characters include such information as the domestic bank account number, branch location identifier, and additional routing information.

While the IBAN concept has taken hold effectively throughout the continent of Europe, it is not a universal global standard yet, though it is the closest thing to one. The practice of working with such standardized account numbers as these is growing and gaining in popularity in other countries of the world. This is proven by the fact that nearly forty non- European countries now employ the International Bank Account Number system for themselves on only the twentieth anniversary of the concept being introduced originally.

Before the rise of the IBAN, every country utilized its own national standard to identify bank accounts within their own borders. This proved to be confusing in Europe, particularly as the borders between the 27 different EU countries began to blur thanks to the EU. Free movement of people, capital, and goods meant that money was being drawn from and transferred back and forth between the banks and bank accounts of different European states on an increasingly common basis. Sometimes important and even critical routing information was simply missing from transfers and payments.

SWIFT's routing information does not require transaction specific formats which identify both account numbers and transaction types specifically. This is because they leave the transaction partners to agree on these. SWIFT codes also lack check digits, meaning transcription errors can not be detected nor can banks validate the routing data before they submit the payments without these two digits. Continuous costly routing errors were creating delays on payments and transfers as the receiving and sending banks were also working with intermediary banks for routing.

The ISO International Organization for Standardization overcame these problems in 1997 by creating the IBAN in association with the European Committee for Banking Standards. Because the ECBS simplified and better standardized the original format proposed by the ISO, an update was issued with ISO 13616:2003 and then again in ISO 13616-1:2007.

As of 2017, the United States' banks do not employ IBANs themselves. Instead, they utilize either Fedwire identifiers for the banks or the ABA Routing Number.

Janet Yellen

With her appointment as the first female Chair of the Board of Governors of the Federal Reserve System, Janet Yellen has been hailed as one of the foremost living American economists. She previously served faithfully and effectively as Vice-Chairman of the Fed from 2010 until she rose to the post of head of the Fed with President Barrack Obama's appointment in 2014.

Janet Yellen has a long and distinguished history with the Federal Reserve System that goes back decades before her appointment as Chair of the Board of Governors. She left a teaching career at prestigious Harvard University in order to take up work as an economist at the Federal Reserve in 1977 and 1978.

Janet Yellen departed from this post to become a London School of Economics lecturer in economics and political science, where she taught for nearly three years. After her initial time at the Fed, she then had a 20 year hiatus out of government service while she worked as a University of California, Berkeley professor. In this time, she met and married her husband who also worked as a professor at the school.

In 1997, Janet Yellen again found herself back in Federal Service, this time working on the White House Council of Economic Advisers for President Bill Clinton through 1999. By 2004, Yellen had advanced to become CEO and President of the Federal Reserve Bank of San Francisco. Six years later, the Fed elevated her to serve in the capacity of Vice Chair of the Board of Governors under the leadership of Ben Bernanke. President Barack Obama then nominated her to succeed Bernanke as Chairman of the Board in October of 2013.

While President of the Federal Reserve Bank of San Francisco, Janet Yellen demonstrated unusual perception concerning the country's declining economic status. She both correctly recognized and predicted the 2008 housing crisis, almost alone among the contemporary economists to do so. During her tenure in this position, Yellen became well known as an outspoken champion of utilizing the Federal Reserve's various powers in order to lower unemployment.

Her track record indicates that she is more willing to risk higher inflation than rival economists in successfully accomplishing this difficult higher employment rate task. When the Senate confirmed Janet Yellen to succeed Ben Bernanke in the capacity of Chair of the Board of Governors for the Federal Reserve System on January 6, 2014, she became the only woman to head up the Federal Reserve Board so far.

Yellen's career has been not only long but also distinguished. This has given her ample time to write an exceptionally large volume of publications and papers. She has also co-written some of these with her Nobel Prize award winning economist husband Professor George Akerlof of UC Berkeley.

Janet Yellen has been widely recognized for her countless contributions with the accolades she has received in the field of economics. In the middle 1980s, she received the honor of serving as a Guggenheim Fellow. In 1997, Yale University awarded Yellen with the prestigious Wilbur Lucius Cross Medal.

Though she has argued strenuously in favor of raising historically low interest rates in the United States as Federal Reserve Chair, Janet Yellen has only been able to successfully raise them one time so far as of July 2016. Continuously erupting global economic instability and especially the turmoil resulting from the Brexit leave vote fallout has repeatedly staid her hand otherwise so far. To this point, she has been widely supported by other members of the Federal Reserve System's voting presidents in these controversial holding on interest rate decisions.

JP Morgan Chase

JP Morgan Chase turns out to be among the oldest financial institutions or banks that are based in the United States. The firm's history hails back more than 200 years. Today, the company boasts assets that exceed $2.4 trillion, and it is a leading global banking and financial services outfit. JP Morgan Chase has a presence in over 100 countries and maintains more than 235,000 employees around the globe in over 450 corporate offices.

JP Morgan Chase counts millions of individuals and small businesses as customers of the banking group. They serve some of the most important governments, institutions, and corporations in the world. JP Morgan proves to be one of the global leaders in financial services for individuals and small businesses, investment banking, commercial banking, asset management, and financial transactions and processing. One of their proudest achievements as a testament to their importance in the United States is the fact that their company stock is one of the only 30 company components of the famed Dow Jones Industrial Average.

JP Morgan Chase & Company proves to be not only one of the oldest and biggest financial institutions in the world, but also among the best known such organizations on earth. The earliest predecessor of the banking group received its charter in New York City in 1799. The company has an aggressive history of mergers and acquisitions that have seen over 1,200 predecessor banking and financial institutions merged into the present day form of the banking behemoth.

Among its most important legacy firms are J.P. Morgan, Chase Manhattan Bank, Chemical Bank, and Manufacturers Hanover of New York City as well as Bank One, National Bank of Detroit, and First Chicago in the Midwest. These institutions each held important ties for their day and age to progress in finance and the expansion of both the American and world economies.

The mega mergers of the banking group began in 2000 when J.P. Morgan & Co. Inc. merged together with the Chase Manhattan Corporation. In this merger, J.P. Morgan, Chase, Manufacturers Hanover, and Chemical became one enormous financial conglomerate. This at last combined four of the biggest, most important, and oldest banking center groups of New

York City together under the single entity name and ownership of J.P. Morgan Chase & Co.

The activity continued in 2004. J.P. Morgan Chase & Company merged with Chicago's Bank One Corporation. At the time, the New York Times newspaper claimed that the combination would remake the competitive landscape of banking as it tied together the commercial and investment banking prowess of J.P. Morgan Chase with the significant consumer banking abilities of the Midwestern-based Bank One.

In 2008, JP Morgan Chase acquired the world's largest savings and loan Washington Mutual Bank as a result of the biggest bank failure in history. Gaining control of Washington Mutual's substantial banking operations meant that the banking group expanded its consumer branches into Florida, California, and Washington State for the first time. This formed the second biggest network of bank locations in the United States whose branches reached an astonishing 42% of all people living in the U.S.

That same year in the depths of the financial crisis, JP Morgan Chase took over the collapsing Wall Street firm The Bear Stearns Companies. This improved the group's swelling abilities in a wide variety of businesses such as global energy trading, cash clearing, and prime brokerage. The group rounded out its presence in the United Kingdom in 2010 by gaining full ownership of its original British joint venture J.P. Morgan Cazenove. This joint venture was among the most premier investment banks in Britain.

Lloyds Banking Group

Lloyds Banking Group represents the biggest financial services consortium in the United Kingdom. As a financial services provider that concentrates on business and retail clients, they count millions of customers throughout the country. They have a presence in practically every community of the U.K.

Part of the impressive size and strength of Lloyds Banking Group centers on its major household name brands. Among the most important of these are Lloyds Bank, Bank of Scotland, Halifax, and Scottish Widows.

The main businesses of the Lloyds Banking Group help it to touch so many customers in their daily lives. They provide retail, business, and corporate banking. The group also delivers general and life insurance. They provide investment opportunities and pension plans as well.

The shares of the Lloyds Banking Group trade on the London Stock Exchange as well as the New York Stock Exchange. The company is one of the biggest in the main British stock market benchmark index the FTSE 100. It also ranks among the largest banks in the world.

Lloyds Banking Group also runs the biggest retail bank in the United Kingdom. This was formerly known as Lloyds TSB but is now simply called Lloyds Bank. It claims the highest number of bank branches in the country. This gives them access to a diversified and massive base of customers. It helps them to cross sell products and services so that they are able to offer a total package of financial services and products for their clients. Their mobile, telephone, and digital services are comprehensive.

The history of this leading member in the Lloyds Banking Group, Lloyds Bank, goes back three centuries. Founded in 1765, the bank celebrated its 250 year anniversary back in 2015. This also makes it among the oldest of the largest banks in the world.

Lloyds Bank started its first branch in Birmingham where it operated as a single branch for a hundred years. In the twentieth century, it pursued decades of mergers to grow into first a national and then an international bank. The 1995 merger with TSB changed its name to Lloyds TSB Bank for a time. In the process of its expansion, the bank gained control of the company which invented Travelers Checks, opened the first British ATM machine, and had a foremost part in launching among the first credit cards in the United Kingdom.

Bank of Scotland is headquartered in Edinburgh. It turns out to be the oldest bank in Scotland. The Scottish Parliament founded it in 1695. It has remained a cornerstone of Scottish business since the act created it. The Parliament originally established the bank to increase the trade of Scotland with nearby trading partners. These included neighboring England and the Low Countries (now Belgium, the Netherlands, and Luxembourg).

The Bank of Scotland also claims a number of pioneering firsts in the industry. It became the very first European commercial bank to issue banknotes with success. It continues to do this today. The bank became the first in the U.K. to put in a computer for processing accounts in 1959. In 2009 the bank joined the Lloyds Group.

The banking group also owns the Halifax brand. This is a building society that arose in 1852. A little group set it up in meetings at the Halifax based Old Cock Inn. They created this investment and loan society to benefit the area working people. Individuals with extra money were able to invest it while others could borrow these funds to build or buy their own house. Eventually Halifax grew into the largest building society around the globe. It counts over 18 million customers today.

Monte dei Paschi di Sienna Bank

Monte dei Paschi di Sienna Bank is the oldest bank in Italy, Europe, and the world. It is also among the most important financial institutions in Italy as the third largest Italian bank. As the flagship brand of the MPS Group (Monte Paschi Sienna), it leads the domestic market and lending market in market share percentages. It trades on the country's most impressive and respected index, the FTSE MIB in Milan, the nation's financial center.

The bank is affectionately known as "il Monte" by millions of Italians who are customers, investors, or creditors to it around the country. Founded in 1472 by merchants in the then Republic of Sienna, the bank has evolved into the ideal reminder of the once-glorious medieval banking and mercantile traditions of both Sienna and the formerly independent Italian city states.

Unfortunately for Monte dei Paschi di Sienna Bank, the world's oldest lending institution has lost its luster and is no longer solvent. Il Monte's financial woes began back in the wake of the American-bank caused financial crisis of 2007. Since then, the Monte dei Paschi di Sienna Bank has announced bad loans to the tune of an eye-watering 28 billion Euros (almost $30 billion US). It has been recapitalized three previous times and yet still desperately trying to secure 5 billion Euros in new capital in order to fund continuing operations. As of end of December 2016, the bank had failed to successfully come up with more than half that amount. Its shares ceased trading on the Italian stock market on the news on December 22nd, as Italian lawmakers urgently approved a 20 billion Euros rescue package fund for the listing bank.

Despite the fact that European Union regulations frown on public bank bailouts since the banking law reforms enacted following the financial and European Sovereign Debt crises, Italy is doggedly pursuing such a rescue. The reason is because of contagion fears to the rest of the Italian banking system, which may easily also spread beyond the national boundaries into the continental European bank powerhouses of embattled German largest financial institution Deutsche Bank, French titans BNP Paribas and Societe Generale, and Swiss behemoths UBS and Credit Suisse.

The Italian banking system is critically important because it is the life blood of the third largest economy in the Euro Zone. Italy is at the same time the second biggest debt to GDP ratio holder in Europe. This is also a scary concern for investors, who know all too well that Italy is the world's third largest sovereign bond market after the United States and Japan. Millions of investors and financial institutions in Italy, the EU, the U.S., and the rest of the world even have exposure to the Italian government bond markets. Besides this, Italy is a member of the G7 great nation economies of the world, with a trillion dollar plus economy whose health and financial future has a very material impact on both the EU and the world economy as a whole.

The global economy can not survive an Italian banking crisis. Italy has become too big to fail as a nation. Italy's largest bank Unicredito remains one of the world's systemically critical global banks. Yet the country is fully in a banking crisis anyway you look at the situation. If Monte dei Paschi di Sienna Bank can not be saved, the resulting Italian banking system crash could cause the entire Euro zone to unwind and the world economy to enter yet another Great Recession as in 2007-2009.

Despite feeble attempts to curb their government debt, the Italian government has only watched it grow to 133 percent of their entire GDP. The most current Bank of Italy provided data proved that the nation's total public debt increased to an astonishing 2.22 trillion through October 2016. With this enormous public debt burden saddling down Italy, the nation faces a literal ticking time bomb thanks to the boiling bank crisis.

This is why the fate of Monte dei Paschi di Sienna may rule the futures of not only its countless Italian pensioner investors and creditors, but also citizens of the whole world. Two decades before Christopher Columbus found the Americas, the bank that holds the key to the stability of the world banking system today first arose. Now the venerable Tuscan-based lender is threatening to overturn the very Western world economies it helped to usher into the modern era of banking and finance as people know it today.

National Bank Act

The National Bank Act refers to three different congressionally passed acts which set up a regime of national banks for the disparate state banks across the United States. These three Federal Banking Acts enabled the U.S. National Banking System to arise. The idea was to foster the creation of a nationwide currency which would be backed up by U.S. Treasury securities held by banks.

The Office of the Comptroller of the Currency under the umbrella of the U.S. Department of the Treasury wanted to be the sole issuer of American currency. To this effect, Treasury authorized the Comptroller of the Currency to start examining and regulating the nationally chartered U.S. banks. These series of acts were responsible for determining the system of national banks in place today and supporting a cohesive banking policy for the United States as a whole.

The first such effort to create a central bank since the First and Second Banks of the United States had failed began with the National Bank Act of 1863. This became the model which was used in the Federal Reserve Act of 1913 eventually. This first act permitted national banks to be created, gave the Federal government permission to sell securities and war bands, and established a plan for creating a unified national currency backed up by government securities.

The Federal government itself directly chartered these subsequent national banks which became subjected to tighter regulation than other banks were at the time. The national banks had to maintain larger capital requirements and could not loan out in excess of 10 percent of their total deposits. The government discovered they could discourage the competition by levying a burdensome tax on the state banks. It only took until 1865 for the majority of the state banks to apply for national charters or to fail altogether.

In 1864, the Federal government waded into the realm of active supervision of all commercial banks. They did this using the National Bank Act of 1864, which was itself based on a law from New York State. This important act created the Office of the Comptroller of the Currency. This office carried the responsibility for chartering, supervising, and examining every national bank.

A year later Congress added still more to this new legislation in the form of the Banking Act of 1865. This July 13, 1866 passed legislation expanded the law to more than simply mandating a 10 percent tax on all of their own state bank proprietary notes. It extended the tax from state banks, national banking associations, and state banking associations so that individuals who utilized such proprietary state bank notes would also be subjected to an additional 10 percent tax.

The act became challenged and subsequently strengthened as a result of the court case known as *Veazie* Bank versus *Fenno*, supra. Thanks to the Chief Justices of the Supreme Court electing to rule with Congress on the matter, all final resistance offered by the state banks to the National Bank Acts of 1865-1866 collapsed.

The 10 percent taxed proved to be so onerous that the majority of state banks chose to change their charters for national ones in order to sidestep the heavy handed tax. This led to the decline for a few years of state banks. In the 1870's and 1880's, state banks saw a resurgence once again as state bank created checks allowed them to get around the failing profitability and importance of their own proprietary bank notes.

Offshore Account

Offshore accounts are accounts that you have in a bank that is located in another country. The term originally came from banks and accounts that were found in the Channel Islands, which were literally off shore from Great Britain. Interestingly enough, the majority of offshore banks and offshore accounts are still found on islands to this day.

Individuals and businesses might use offshore accounts for a variety of purposes. The popular conception of offshore accounts is that spies and criminals utilize them as places to store their cash. In fact, most offshore accounts are completely legitimate. People and even businesses have them as places to deposit their money, make investments, or use as trading accounts. When they are used as trading accounts, the person utilizes them to place online trades in stock markets.

Offshore accounts can also be employed to hide assets from governments and taxes, even though this is not the case for most such offshore accounts. A number of offshore banking accounts exist, such as HSBC Offshore Banking in Gibralter, Barclays Offshore Banking in the island of Jersey, and Griffon Bank in the island of Dominica in the Caribbean. These accounts provide all types of services for the banking needs of people and businesses, one of which is Internet banking.

Among the advantages of offshore accounts is privacy. Offshore banking institutions keep offshore account information secret. Such banks are forbidden to declare this information concerning the status of the account or any of its particulars to any individual or entity who is not the account holder. The only exception to this is when offshore banks believe the holder of an offshore account may be using the account for illegal purposes like drug trafficking, support of terrorism, or criminal money laundering.

Another good reason for putting your money into an offshore bank account is because they typically offer better interest on money. It is a well known fact that offshore banks provide better interest rates for their customers. Such rates depend on the location and the offshore bank in question. Reasons for higher interest rates have to do with the lower operating costs in these islands or other locations, as well as the higher interest rates in the prosperous countries where they are based.

Tax advantages prove to be another motivating factor for offshore banking and having offshore accounts. A number of countries will provide tax benefits to investors who are foreigners in order to attract their money. While this is different for every location too, many offshore banks and their hosting countries will not levy taxes on investment returns and interest earned in such offshore accounts.

Paul Volcker

Paul Volcker is the former Chairman of the Board of Governors of the Federal Reserve Board who continues to be influential in policy and in an advisory role to the President of the United States. He is one of the few living individuals to have an economic policy rule named after him.

Throughout his lengthy career of public service, Volcker has worked for the U.S. Federal Government for nearly 30 years. He became Chairman of the Federal Reserve from 1979 to 1987. Besides this, the man split his earlier career between the Treasury Department, Federal Reserve Bank of New York, and Chase Manhattan Bank.

It was President Jimmy Carter who elevated Paul Volcker to the role as Chairman of the Federal Reserve in 1979. He did a quality job and received reappointment from President Ronald Reagan in 1983. During his tenure in the big chair at the Fed, Volcker was forced to fight 10% yearly inflation. He did so using controversial contractionary monetary policy. This took real courage, as he had to double the Federal Funds rate from an already high 10.25% in 1979 to 20% by March of 1980.

After tinkering with the rates up and down for a year, Volcker maintained them at over 16% through May of 1981. This period of stunningly high interest rates became known as the Volcker Shock. It served its intended purpose to stop the inflation in the U.S. Regrettably, it also directly led to the recession of 1981.

The Volcker shock worked once Paul Volcker successfully convinced businesses and members of the public that he was serious in his unparalleled action to tame inflation. Former President Richard Nixon had caused the inflation when he abandoned the gold standard back in 1973. He crashed the value of the dollar and promoted inflation in the process. Nixon's futile efforts to stop the inflation by instituting wage-price controls in 1971 only led to slower growth with continued inflation that became known as stagflation.

Fed chairman of the day Alfred Hayes lowered and raised interest rates like a see-saw in his efforts to defeat Nixon's inflation and recession simultaneously. In the end this simply confused businesses and consumers about what Fed policy really was. After the end of wage-price controls in 1972, businesses increased their prices to try to keep ahead of higher interest rates. Consumers also participated by purchasing more goods before firms could again raise prices. The Fed had lost all credibility. Inflation attained double digits as things spiraled out of control.

Paul Volcker was responsible for helping global central bankers to understand how import it was to manage expectations regarding inflation. He had forced consumers to stop their runaway spending habits when they understood that he was serious about beating inflation. Businesses similarly quit raising their prices, and this put an end to high inflation.

Paul Volcker served in a variety of important capacities after retiring as head of the Fed. He led a committee looking into Swiss bank held assets of Nazi victims from 1996 to 1999. He worked as the International Accounting Standards Committee Chairman from 2000 to 2005 where he helped to create an international accounting standard that all nations could uphold.

In 2004 he chaired the Independent Inquiry into the United Nations' scandalized Oil-for-Food Program. President Obama again called on the expert services of Paul Volcker in November of 2008 as he asked him to head up the President's Economic Recovery Advisory Board. Eight years later, he remains Chairman of the Board (as of 2016). In this capacity, he fought for and achieved stricter banking regulations that became known as the Volcker Rule.

Rabobank

Rabobank refers to the Dutch banking giant whose full name is the Coöperatieve Rabobank. This Dutch international banking giant is a full-scale financial services organization whose headquarters today lies in the city of Utrecht in the Netherlands. The banking group is a world leader for agriculture and food production financing as well as in banking based on sustainability. Their motto is "as large as necessary, as small as possible."

The group Rabobank is a unique form of banking organization and structure in many ways. It is made up of 120 fully independent local Rabobanks in the Netherlands as of 2013. These banks actually own the parent central organization called Rabobank Nederland. They also operate a significant number of subsidiaries and specialized international operations and offices. The main international concentration of the Rabobank Group proves to be agribusiness and food-related.

By their assets, this bank remains the second biggest Dutch bank. When measured by their Tier 1 Capital, the bank proves to be in the top 30 biggest financial institutions on earth. Current as of December 2014, their aggregate assets equaled 681 billion (Euros) while they claimed a net profit amount of 1.8 billion. The banking and finance industry publication Global Finance ranks Rabobank at an impressive number 25 for "world's safest banks."

The bank's historical and current day roots remain in agriculture. As a confederation of local credit union banks which deliver banking and financial services to their local markets, the company operates on a bottom up model which is most unusual in banking. This means that the central organization and all of its countless subsidiaries and international offices throughout the world are a huge subsidiary of the local Dutch branches. With the overwhelming majority of commercial banks in the world today, the central organization proves to be the owning parent entity.

The roots of the bank came from the founder of the credit union cooperative movement Friedrich Wilhelm Raiffeisen, whose name is today immortalized in the enormous central and Eastern European, Austrian-based Raiffeisen Bank. He was the one who started the original farmers' bank within Germany. The local countryside town mayor was aghast at the dire poverty he saw in the local farmers, their families, and communities. Though he attempted to deliver charity to alleviate their suffering, he soon discovered that helping them to be more self-reliant would yield better results over the long term. He did this by establishing his farmers' banks which gathered up the countryside residents' savings in order to offer them out as loans to enterprising farmers who needed capital to expand. Among his early followers was Father Gerlacus van den Elsen. He founded and inspired many of the local farmers' banks throughout the south of the Netherlands.

The bank had traditional dual headquarters in both Utrecht and Eindhoven. It was in the year 1898 that two different cooperative banking conglomerates formed as the Utrecht- based Coöperatieve Centrale Raiffeisen-Bank and the Eindhoven-based Coöperatieve Centrale Boerenleenbank. The former proved to be a co-op of six different area banks, while the latter existed when 22 local banks formed their co-op. Even though the two banks were largely the same, they still operated as separate competitors alongside one another for around 75 years. It was ironically the differing Christian religious bents of the two banks that kept them apart for so long. While the Eindhoven co-op was strongly Catholic, the Utrecht based Raiffeisen-Bank had Protestant roots. It explained why the Catholic based-bank was heavily centralized while the Protestant-based bank encouraged local autonomy of its branches.

The two were cooperating by 1940 and merged together in 1972 as Rabobank. The name changed to Rabobank Nederland in 1980. Overseas expansion came through many acquisitions in farming-oriented countries. They bought Primary Industry Bank of Australia in 1994 and reformed this as Rabobank Australia Limited by 2003. In 1997 they acquired Wrightson Farmers Finance Limited of New Zealand and converted this in 1999 to Rabobank New Zealand. They entered Indonesia decisively with the buyout of Bank Haga and Bank Hagakita. In 2011 and 2012, they opened online banks in Poland and then Germany. A savings business in Ireland followed. They also expanded into the Western U.S. with the purchase of Mid-State Bank & Trust in 2007 and Pacific State Bank in 2010.

Repayment Penalty

A repayment penalty is commonly associated with paying back a loan before the end of its term. If you are contemplating paying off your loan balance in advance of its due date, then you should be aware that a number of loans come with these repayment penalties for liquidating the balance early. Different types of loans utilize different names for these same fees. Repayment penalties can also be called redemption charges, early redemption fees, prepayment penalties, or financial penalties.

The fees associated with repayment penalties vary depending on the loan in question. These repayment penalties are commonly stated as a percentage of the balance that is outstanding when prepayment is offered. Alternatively, they might be figured up as a certain number of months of interest charges. In general, when they are figured up using months of interest, they are comprised of one to two months' interest in fees. The sooner in the loan's life that you choose to repay the loan, the greater amount of charge you can expect to pay. This is because the anticipated interest portion of the loan comprises a great part of the repayment earlier in the loan's time frame. Early repayment penalties might increase the total cost of your loan significantly.

If you wish to avoid a repayment penalty in paying off your loan in advance of the term's end, then you will have to be aware of the loans that come with these fees and the ones that do not. Even if you change a currently existing loan into a loan for debt consolidation, you will have to cover the early repayment penalty if one is in the terms. The only way to avoid early repayment penalties is by selecting loans that specifically do not have ones attached to them. It is ironic that some of the least expensive loans out there do not include repayment penalties for early pay off actions.

Another factor of repayment penalties involves a gradual disappearance of the provision over time. With many mortgages, these repayment penalties gradually go down over the years of the mortgage. After the fifth year, the majority of repayment penalties no longer even apply. In many cases, repayments of as much as twenty percent of the original balance are permitted in a given year without you having to be penalized.

Besides this, there are different kinds of penalties for repayments. Penalties that only apply to your refinancing of the mortgage are called soft penalties. Penalties that include the sale of the house and a refinancing are known as hard penalties.

Retail Banking

Retail banking is also called consumer banking. This form of banking is most easily described as the common everyday activities of financial service firms. In this definition their individual clientele utilize the local area branches of the more significant and bigger commercial banks. They provide a wide range of services to their customers through this division of financial services. These include checking and savings accounts, personal loans, mortgages for homes, lines of credit, credit cards and debit cards, and CDs certificates of deposits investment opportunities for customers. The main concentration is on the one on one consumer relationship.

Within the United States, the phrase commercial bank refers to a traditional bank. This term distinguishes it from the competing concept of investment bank. Following the Great Depression of the 1930s, the American Congress mandated that banks were only allowed to participate in traditional deposit and lending banking activities as opposed to investment activities. This Glass Steagall Act similarly required that investment banks could only participate in activities pertaining to the capital markets.

This important separation prevented another severe financial crisis like the Great Depression from erupting. Unfortunately for Americans everywhere, the Congress chose to repeal these protections afforded to markets and individuals by Glass Steagall when they canceled out the act in the 1990s. This allowed commercial banks to once again dabble in investment bank activities with depositors' money. It was considered to be a main factor which led to the financial collapse of the Great Recession in the years 2007-2009.

Commercial banking also relates to a division of a bank, or even an entire bank, that focuses on larger businesses and corporations. They handle these huge entities' loans and deposits. This would separate the concept from retail banking which only addresses the ordinary individuals along with their banking needs and accounts.

The idea behind retail banking is to be a one size fits all, single stop shop which provides all the financial services which they possibly can to their retail customers. Bank clients demand a full lineup of essential banking services from these retail operations. Included in this are such expected products as savings and checking accounts, lines of credit, personal loans, home loans, credit cards, debit cards, and CDs. The majority of retail banking customers visits their local bank branch in order to receive these services. Such centers deliver the consumer demanded onsite client service to provide for each of these retail customer requirements.

Financial representatives also work in these local area branches. They offer their clients of the bank both financial advice and customer service. Such financial reps prove to be the primary contact for garnering credit related applications for these products which help the banks to generate their revenues and profits.

These types of banks have begun to offer expanded retail services so that they can capture more business from their retail customers. Besides the typical bank accounts and accompanying customer service that the in branch financial reps deliver, banking centers have added various combinations of financial advisors. They provide a wide array of product offerings. Some of these are investment services like stock brokerage accounts, wealth management services, retirement planning, and even private banking for High Net Worth Individual clients and families.

There are occasionally insurance products and services offered through the in-branch retail banking network as well. Sometimes, such ancillary products and services will be provided out of third party affiliated institutions like insurance companies and investment firms. The idea behind such broadened offerings is to both provide customers greater convenience and to develop more points of financial interaction between them and the bank. This allows for clients of the bank to have greater and more convenient access to their funds and to engage in personal banking transactions both faster and easier.

The Internet has also made possible online retail banking. Many banks now offer partial banking services online. A few are actually banks which are entirely structured to provide banking services over the Internet alone. Among these are GoBank, Moven, and Simple. They offer lower fees as they have significantly smaller overheads with no in-branch personnel, buildings, and networks to support.

The top five biggest American commercial banks possessed more than half of the retail bank customer deposits for the entire country in the year 2015. These five largest institutions were JPMorgan, Bank of America/Merrill Lynch, Wells Fargo, Citibank, and U.S. Bank.

Run on the Bank

A run on the bank is the vernacular expression for a bank run. Runs on the banks actually happen as a result of many bank customers deciding to take out their deposits at one time. They do this out of fear that the bank is either broke or on its way to becoming insolvent. When runs on the banks get started, they have a tendency to create their own terrible momentum that leads to a self fulfilling prophecy. The more customers who take out their money, the greater the odds of bank default become, which leads to still more customer deposit withdrawals. If this happens long enough, it will likely upset a bank's finances to the point that the bank encounters bankruptcy as a result.

Runs on the bank can often lead to bank panics. These financial crises result from a large number of banks experiencing bank runs all at once. If the bank panics are not dealt with swiftly and convincingly, then a systemic banking crisis can develop. In such a banking crisis that is system wide, it is not uncommon to witness practically all, or even all, of a country's banking capital disappear.

Once this occurs, numerous bankruptcies follow, many times ending up in a deep and painful economic recession or even depression. Bank runs created a great amount of the economic damage that you saw done in the Great Depression. Associated costs of fixing the mess related to a systemic banking crisis are enormous. Over the last forty years, these expenses around the world have averaged fully thirteen percent of the respective countries' Gross Domestic Products in fiscal costs, leading to losses of economic output that averaged twenty percent of Gross Domestic Product.

Runs on the bank are able to be prevented with a few different strategies. Withdrawals can be suspended. More effectively, deposit insurance systems can be put in place, like the one that the Federal Deposit Insurance Corporation operates in the United States. The Central Bank may also help out banks by performing the function of the lender of last resort in times of banking crises. Such strategies are commonly effective, but not always. Even when countries possess deposit insurance, the bank depositors could still be fearful that they will not have instant access to their bank held deposits while the bank is reorganized by the FDIC.

The reason that runs on the bank are able to happen in the first place is because of the fractional reserve banking system. Modern day banks only keep a small percentage of their demand deposits in cash on hand, typically ten percent in developed nations. The rest of these deposits are tied up in loans that have longer terms than demand deposits. This leads to a mismatch of assets and liabilities. Though some banks keep better reserves than others do, no modern bank keeps sufficient reserves in its vaults to handle the majority of their deposits being withdrawn at a single time.

Short Sale

Short sales are real estate sales where the money received from the sale is not sufficient to cover the balance that is owed on the property loan. This commonly happens as a result of borrowers being unable to keep up with the mortgage payments for their home loan. In this case, the bank or other lending institution will likely determine that it is in their best interest to take a reasonable loss on the sale of the property instead of pressuring the borrower to make the payments that he or she can not afford.

Both parties come together and agree on the short sale process, since it permits them both to stay out of foreclosure. Foreclosure is a negative outcome for the two parties, as it lowers credit scores of borrowers and costs banks in expensive fees. Borrowers must be careful, since a short sale agreement does not always absolve the borrower from having to cover the additional balance left on the loan. This remaining balance is called the deficiency.

The process of a short sale starts with the two parties concurring on a short sale being the best option to resolve a mortgage that the borrower is unable to keep up with as a result of financial or economic difficulties. The home owner actually sells the house in question for an amount that he or she is able to realize, even though it is less than the remaining loan balance. They give the money to the bank or lender. This is really the most economical answer for the problem in this scenario, since short sales are less costly and quicker than foreclosures that damage both lender and borrower.

Banks commonly employ loss mitigation departments. Their job is to contemplate the short sales that are possible or likely. Most of them work with criteria that they have set up in advance. In the difficult days following the financial crisis of 2007-2010, they have become more flexible and willing to entertain offers from borrowers. The banks will usually decide on how much equity is in the house by ascertaining the likely selling price that they will be able to receive either through a Broker Price Opinion, appraisal, or Broker Opinion of Value.

Even when Notice of Defaults have been sent out to borrowers beginning a foreclosure process, many banks will still consent to short sale requests and offers. They have become more understanding and accepting of short sales in the wake of the financial crisis than they ever were before. This means that for the countless borrowers who own houses on which they owe more than they are worth and who can not sell them, there is a better option open to them than foreclosure.

Sub-prime Mortgage

A sub-prime mortgage is one where the home loan that the bank or lending institution makes is offered to the category of consumers who are considered to possess the riskiest credit. Sub prime mortgages are actually sold on a different market than are prime mortgage loans. Sub prime mortgage borrowers are determined through a combination of factors, such as the credit rating of the borrower, the documentation offered for the loans, and the borrower's debt to assets ratio. Besides this, sub-prime mortgage are also deemed to be those that do not fulfill the prime mortgages' standards and guide lines offered by Fannie Mae and Freddie Mac, the two biggest issuers of mortgages within the United States.

A universally agreed upon definition for sub-prime mortgages does not exist today. In the U.S., sub-prime mortgages are commonly considered to be those where the associated borrower possesses a FICO credit rating score that is less than 640. This phrase became a part of pop culture in the credit crunch that occurred in 2007.

The original sub-prime mortgage program began in 1993. At this time, some lenders started offering sub-prime mortgages to borrowers classified as high risk, who possessed credit that was less than ideal. Traditional lenders showed wariness towards sub-prime mortgages and borrowers. They tended to shy away from people who had impaired credit histories. Sub-prime mortgage borrowers commonly have information on their credit reports that argue for greater percentages of defaults. These include too much debt, a track record of not paying debts or missing payments, recorded bankruptcies, and low amounts of experience with debt.

Around twenty-five percent of the American population is grouped into this category of sub-prime borrowers who qualify for the category of sub-prime mortgages. Because of this, proponents of sub-prime mortgages argued that they allowed a large number of people to gain access to credit who would not otherwise have experienced the opportunity to purchase and own a home. Borrowers with less than perfect credit who can demonstrate enough income are able to qualify for sub-prime mortgages. This proves to be the case even if their credit scores are lower than 640.

The lenders who participate in sub-prime mortgages take significant risks in so doing. This is because people who have a credit score of less than 620 statistically possess a significantly greater rate of defaulting on their mortgages than do those people with much higher scores over 720. Lenders compensate for the risks associated with offering sub-prime mortgages through several different means. One of these is by charging higher rates of interest. They also collect late fees for any customers who do not keep up with their payments. These greater interest rates and fees help to reward lenders who take the risks of the higher default rates, and who also incur costs for collecting and keeping up with these -mortgage accounts. As an example of their potential danger, sub-prime mortgages proved to be among the main causes of the Financial Crisis of 2007-2010.

SWIFT

SWIFT Network is the internationally relied upon system for transferring money. It underlies the overwhelming majority of security and international money transfers. This vast network for financial messaging is employed by financial institutions such as banks to rapidly, securely, and accurately receive and send information that includes instructions for money transfers. In any given day, almost 10,000 different member institutions of the SWIFT system deploy around 24 million unique financial messages throughout this truly impressive worldwide network.

SWIFT is an acronym that actually means the Society for Worldwide Interbank Financial Telecommunications. This messaging network securely transmits both instructions and sensitive information for financial institutions using a standardized operating system of codes. In order for this amazing system to work, SWIFT itself gives a one of a kind identification code to every financial institution in the world which participates. These codes are comprised of either 11 or eight characters. Names for this code range from SWIFT Code and SWIFT ID to BIC bank identifier code and ISO 9362 code. It should not be confused with the similar yet still different IBAN International Bank Account Number.

An example of one such SWIFT code for a member institution is helpful to look at in order to better understand how SWIFT puts these identifiers together. Consider UniCredit Banca based in Milan, Italy. The eight character SWFT code for UniCredit Banca proves to be UNCRITMM, which stands for UNI CREDIT ITALY Milan (Milan is identified with two Ms). SWIFT always takes the first four letters from the institution's name, making up the institute code. The second two letters are the national code. The next two characters represent the city location code. Another optional three characters stand for the individual branch within a large bank, as in using ZZZ to represent a particular branch location.

Thought SWIFT is undoubtedly a powerful institution and system in the world today, it does not ever hold or touch any securities or cash. It also never manages accounts for clients. Instead it is simply a financial transaction messaging system. Yet this service is critical in today's fast moving world of finance, business, and banking.

This is because the world before SWIFT was a ponderous place in which to do international wire and bank transfers. Before the advent of SWIFT, there was only the Telex system to send the international wire transfer message confirmations. Telex was fraught with problems. Among these were it had security issues, was terribly slow, and lacked a unifying system of standardized codes as SWIFT possesses for naming both the banks and the types of financial transactions being conducted.

A sender with Telex was forced to detail out each and every transaction utilizing sentences that had to be first interpreted then executed by the receivers on the other end. As these people often spoke other languages besides the lingua franca English, it led to countless human errors and mistakes in ultimate transmission.

In order to get around these many problems, seven of the biggest international financial institutions came together to create a cooperative society and system whose entire reason of being was to run a global financial network with would relay such critical financial messages utilizing both speedy and secure means. It only took SWIFT three years to grow rapidly from the original seven founding banks to 230 banks in five nations.

Despite the fact that competing financial messaging services such as FedWire, CHIPS, and Ripple exist, SWIFT has continued to enjoy its now-dominant market share and position. Many observers have noted that this stems in large part from the way it constantly comes up with newer message codes for various financial transactions.

Besides the simplified payment instructions SWIFT arose to deliver, the network additionally delivers messages for a significant and broad-based number of treasury and security transactions throughout the globe. Almost half of the SWIFT worldwide traffic still stems from the traditional heart of the network, the payment messages. An impressive 43 percent today pertain to security transactions. The other under ten percent deals with treasury transactions.

SWIFT has continued to evolve and grow into other related businesses. Today it also deploys its lengthy data maintenance history to deliver reference data, business intelligence, and compliance information services. An area it is addressing now is the delivery and implementation of software automation for its financial transaction messaging system. The company has successfully created and tested such software, but its use and deployment will come at a higher cost to participating banks.

Swiss Banking

Swiss Banking is unusually concentrated into two main banks. These are UBS and Credit Suisse. Together they control an enormous amount of the accounts and assets in all of Switzerland.

The Swiss Banking tradition used to be shrouded in secrecy. Under the administration of American President Obama, many Swiss banks were investigated and charged with helping Americans to illegally evade taxes. This is not a crime in Switzerland, and the country's laws had long protected their banks for engaging in the activity.

Starting with justice probes that investigated around a dozen of these Swiss banking outfits, the U.S. began handing out sentences and fines in 2013. Two banks at least were destroyed by the legal wrangling with the United States' justice department. These included Wegelin & Company and Bank Frey.

Wegelin & Company proved to be the oldest existing Swiss bank when the fines came out. It was the first foreign or Swiss bank to receive a criminal sentence and penalty for helping Americans to avoid taxes. The U.S. Justice Department levied $74 million in fines and forfeitures against the bank. The bank was already being wound down by the Swiss authorities because it had suffered so much financially from the struggle with the American government.

Bank Frey & Co was a boutique lender in the Swiss banking tradition. Its principal office was on the most important banking street in Zurich. In October of 2013 it had to close its doors as well in large part because of the lengthy and costly tax dispute with the U.S.

The main players in Swiss banking today UBS and Credit Suisse operate under similar models as universal Swiss banks with important overseas operations. UBS as the larger of the two has a greater number of banking assets. It is headquartered in Zurich and Basel and boasts operations in over fifty countries. It maintains more than 60,000 employees around the globe. It has offices in every major financial center of the world. About a third of the bank employees work in the Americas division. Slightly more than another third call Switzerland their base of operations.

In just over 150 years of history, UBS has managed to expand and acquire more than 300 different banks. They have over 300 branches and more than 4,500 employees in Switzerland alone. Over a third of all Swiss homes and 120,000 Swiss companies call UBS their bank. Their reach extends to 80% of all the wealth of the Swiss.

Credit Suisse is the second largest Swiss bank in the world after UBS. The bank dates back to 1856. Since then it has grown immensely to achieve a global presence. The bank counts operations in more than 50 different nations. It employs over 48,000 staff who hail from in excess of 150 different countries. In 2006, it started operating as a globally integrated universal bank.

This broad footprint has enabled both banks to create a well balanced revenue stream and to capture many new assets geographically. It provides them with significant opportunities to grow throughout the globe today.

The Credit Suisse and UBS strategies work off the banks' three critical strong positions. They are both leaders in worldwide wealth management. The banks are also standouts for specific investment banking abilities and skills. Finally they have a powerful regional footprint in the home nation of Switzerland.

The banks employ a well balanced strategy of gaining opportunities for wealth management in key emerging markets. This largest focus for them centers on the most important growth area of Asia Pacific. They also strive to serve critical already developed markets while focusing on the original country Switzerland.

Toxic Assets

Toxic Assets is a coined phrase for those financial assets which saw their actual value plummet. Toxic assets do not have well working markets anymore, making them difficult or impossible to sell for a price on which the owner will agree. The term arose as a popularly coined phrase during the financial crisis of 2007-2010. Toxic assets proved to have a major part in causing the financial crisis.

As toxic assets' markets seize up, they are called frozen markets. Many markets for these toxic assets froze up starting in 2007. The problem only continued to grow exponentially worse in the second half of the following year 2008. A number of elements combined to lock up the markets for toxic assets. These assets had values that proved to be extremely vulnerable to the worsening economic situation. As uncertainty only grew in this scenario, finding a value for toxic assets became more difficult. In the resulting frozen markets, banks and similar lending institutions chose not to unload these assets for greatly diminished prices. The reason for it lay in their fear that such drastically lower prices would force them to mark down all of their holdings, so that they became insolvent or bankrupt.

Typically, toxic assets are able to clear when the supply and demand of them reach the point that buyers and sellers will come together. This did not occur in the financial crisis starting in 2007. As a number of the financial assets simply hung around on banks' balance sheets, experts declared that the markets had broken down.

Another way of putting this is that because banks would not write down the prices on the assets, the price of them proved to be overly high. Buyers knew that these assets were now worth far less than the selling banks hoped to realize for them. This kept the sellers' price expectations far higher than buyers were willing to pay.

Toxic assets mostly arose as a result of banks and other investment banks deciding to pour enormous sums of money into new and complex financial assets like credit default swaps and collateralized debt obligations. These highly leveraged assets had values that turned out to be extremely vulnerable to a variety of economic conditions like the rates of default, prices of houses, and liquidity of financial markets. These toxic assets threatened to destroy the entire financial system and did manage to take down a number of venerable institutions like Bear Stearns, Lehman Brothers, and Washington Mutual Bank, the country's largest savings and loan institution. As a result of the carnage created by these highly leveraged, speculative investments in toxic assets, experts have named them financial weapons of mass destruction.

Troubled Asset Relief Program (TARP)

The Troubled Asset Relief Program is also known by its clever acronym the TARP. This represented a series of national relief programs which the United States Treasury Department developed and administered. They did this to attempt to restore stability to the American financial system, to rebuild economic stability and growth, and to forestall housing foreclosures after the 2008 Global Financial Crisis and Great Recession wrecked the national and Western portion of the global economy. The idea was to buy up threatened firms' equity and toxic assets so that they could continue to operate and make loans.

In the first round, the Troubled Asset Relief Program provided Treasury with an mind boggling $700 billion of purchasing ability with which to purchase the dubious and at that point entirely illiquid MBS mortgage-backed securities as well as additional assets. They were to buy these from systemically important banks and financial institutions with an eye on rebuilding the shattered liquidity of the stricken money markets. It was the congressionally approved Emergency Economic Stabilization Act they passed on October 3rd in 2008 which allowed them to develop the program. With the Dodd-Frank Act for banking reforms, the Congress reduced their $700 billion amount of authorization down to a still-impressive $475 billion.

The series of events that led to this de facto bank bailout originated from the freeze up of the worldwide credit markets that ground to a screeching halt in September of 2008. This became worse as a few of the systemically important financial institutions like American International Group, and the GSE government sponsored enterprises Freddie Mac and Fannie Mae became victims of intense financial trouble. Lehman Brothers' went bankrupt which nearly overthrew the global financial system. At the same time Goldman Sachs and Morgan Stanley altered their charters to evolve into commercial banks which provided them with the backing of the FDIC Federal Deposit Insurance Corporation. This did stabilize the attacks on their two market capitalizations and shore up their capital positions, though it required some time to have effect.

It was with the Troubled Asset Relief Program that the government through the U.S. Treasury was finally able to buy up the root of the crisis, the

Mortgage-backed securities. In decreasing the possible unknown toxic asset losses from the financial institutions which held them, they saved the banking system in not only the United States but likely the entire Western world.

Critics of the Troubled Asset Relief Program called it the largest bank bailout scheme in the history of the world. Without these cash infusions into the important national banks throughout the U.S. though, they would have been unable to continue operating at all. When the program had successfully stabilized the banking system and the too big too fail, systemically all-important banks, and the market had sufficiently calmed down, TARP was allowed to expire on October 3rd of 2010.

Treasury utilized the TARP funds wisely and well. They deployed some of them to make loans, others to invest in companies in need of cash infusions, and still more to guarantee toxic assets like the MBS. They received bonds or shares off of the collapsing financial companies and banks in consideration for this accommodation. The first program was known as the Capital Repurchase Program. In this initiative, Treasury purchased preferred shares of stock in eight major banks. These included Citigroup, Bank of America/Merrill Lynch, Goldman Sachs, Morgan Stanley, Bank of New York Mellon, Wells Fargo, J.P. Morgan Chase, and State Street Bank.

The banks had to provide the government with a full five percent dividend return which had to increase to nine percent in 2013. This gave the banks huge incentive to purchase back their own stock from Treasury before the conclusion of the five year windows. Then-Treasury Secretary Hank Paulson understood the government would make money off of the program in the end as he believed the stock prices of the banks would rebound at least somewhat by or before 2013.

Four other groups and entities would have collapsed without additional help from the Troubled Asset Relief Program and Treasury. Each of these received either direct cash infusions via preferred stock purchases or loans. AIG (the largest insurance company in the world) received $40 billion. Various community banks obtained a collective $92 billion. A number of these did fail in spite of this help. The American Big Three car makers got $80.7 billion collectively. Bank of America and Citigroup also received an additional $45 billion between them. TARP also loaned out $20 billion to the sister TALF program which the Federal Reserve managed.

Though critics heavily maligned the government for saving the banking system and national banks, the bailout did not cost the government anything by the time it had been concluded. In fact, by May of 2016, the banks had paid the government back all of their principal (collectively, despite some failing anyway) plus $25 billion in profits for a total repayment of $275.04 billion.

UniCredit Bulbank

UniCredit Bulbank proves to be the biggest bank in the Republic of Bulgaria. Until 1994, this state-controlled and -operated bank bore the name of the Bulgarian Foreign Trade Bank or BFTB. It was in 2007 that the UniCredit Bulbank became formed when Bulbank, Hebros Bank, and Biochim merged together as individual subsidiaries of UniCredit Group from Italy.

Bulgarian Foreign Trade Bank first arose in 1964 in its headquarters of Sofia, Bulgaria. The at the time completely state-owned and -founded bank held an initial paid in capital of 40 million Bulgarian leva when it opened. This proved to be a large sum of capital in this day and age. At the time under the heyday of the communists in Bulgaria it specialized in foreign finance and foreign trade payments.

The bank realized that to effectively pursue foreign trade and finance, it needed several well placed good international branches. The bank then began to open important representative offices in London, Vienna, and Frankfurt throughout the subsequent decades. In 2015, the operation boasted substantially greater assets amounting to nearly 9 billion Euros and 2015 era equity of nearly 13 billion Euros.

Once Communism collapsed in Bulgaria during the successful national coup in 1989, the country established the Bank Consolidation Company in 1991 to operate the state- controlled banking sector and to help with the eventual privatizing of the various national Bulgarian banks. BCC owned 98 percent of the share capital of Bulbank at the time. It became the first Bulgarian bank operation to change over to international SWIFT codes. This helped it to massively improve its transaction reliability and operational performance as a direct result.

The bank's eventual privatization from 1998 to 2000 saw UniCredito Italiano gain control of 93 percent of the capital shares while German based re-insurance giant Allianz obtained another five percent of the remaining shares. Bulbank then sold its majority stakes in Corporate Commercial Bank and minor stakes in United Bulgarian Bank and HypoVereinsbank Bulgaria.

Bulbank has continuously worked on the merger of operations and branches between the old Bulbank offices and Hebros Bank and HVB Bank Biochim since UniCredit made the decision to merge the HVB Group back in 2005. The group was renamed UniCredit Bulbank officially at this point.

The same Chief Executive Officer has overseen the company's massive successes since the year 2001. This towering figure in Bulgarian banking and finance is Mr. Levon Hampartzoumian. He heads UniCredit Bulbank still as of end of 2016 in its second decade of existence in the present foreign owned-form of the financial institution.

Part of the leading in Bulgaria success that UniCredit Bulbank has consistently enjoyed in recent decades stems from the wide range of clientele they effectively serve. They offer bank checking, current, and savings accounts, insurance and investment products, land and home mortgages, and financing and credit for individual clients, private banking customers, small businesses, large corporate clients, other financial institutions, and even Bulgarian government and other public institutions as well.

UniCredit Bulbank is not only by far and away the largest bank in Bulgaria by branches, deposits, and assets; it is also a heavily award-winning financial institution. In 2016, it received the honors of "Bank of the Year" from the Association Bank of the Year and "Best Bank for 2016" from Global Finance Magazine. It is known as the "Best Digital Bank in Bulgaria for 2016" per Global Finance Magazine. Focus Economics ranks it as the "Most Precise Overall Economic Forecast for Bulgaria." Forbes Magazine labeled it the "Most Innovative Bank in Bulgaria". It received the "Best Bank in Bulgaria" designations from EMEA Finance Magazine and K10's Kapital Newspaper annual ranking. Global Finance Magazine called UniCredit Bulbank the "Best Trade Finance Bank in Bulgaria" in 2016, as did Euromoney Magazine as well.

Volcker Rule

The Volcker Rule is a controversial much loved or intensely hated part of the Frank-Dodd Wall Street Reform and Consumer Protection Act. This federal regulation made it illegal for banks to pursue specific investment activities using their own money and accounts.

It also restricted their relationship to and ownership of private equity funds and hedge funds. These so called covered funds engaged in a variety of speculative leveraged and high risk investments. Such investments and their ultimate massive failures played a major part in the American and ultimately global financial collapse of the 2008 financial crisis and Great Recession.

The Volcker Rule was originally named for Paul Volcker, the one time legendary Federal Reserve Chairman. This rule eliminates short term bank trading of derivatives, securities, commodity futures, and options on such futures. They may no longer use their own accounts for such trading that does not provide any benefit to the customers of the banks. The end result is that banks may not engage their own proprietary funds in order to participate in investments that may boost their own corporate profits.

This Volcker Rule is spelled out under section 619 of the massive Dodd-Frank Wall Street Reform and Consumer Protection Act. It amended the Bank Holding Company Act of 1956, also known as the BHC Act, by adding in a brand new section 13 that has become universally known as the Volcker Rule. All institutions which accept deposits, as well as any corporate entity that is affiliated with these insured depository groups, are prohibited from pursing this secretive proprietary trading.

They also may no longer have an interest in, acquire, or sponsor any private equity or hedge funds. There are some exemptions, definitions, and restrictions in the legal statute. It provided banking groups with some time until they had to prove they had conformed to the provisions of the rule. Originally this was July of 2014, but it was later extended to July 21, 2015 in order to provide banks with sufficient time to extricate themselves from these trades and practices.

The end form of the regulations had to be approved by five different federal agencies. These included the Federal Deposit Insurance Corporation, the Federal Reserve System Board of Governors, The Commodity Futures Trading Commission, the Office of the Comptroller of the Currency, and the SEC Securities and Exchange Commission. They approved these rules in December of 2013.

The rules became effective on April 1, 2014 and required banks' complete compliance by July 21, 2015. The Volcker Rule did not completely tie banks' hands. They are still allowed to keep making markets, hedging, and underwriting government securities. They may also engage in the activities of insurance companies and perform the roles of custodians, brokers, and agents.

They may offer customers private equity funds or hedge funds for their own accounts and benefit. All such services which they provide to their customers they may do in an effort to turn profits. The caveat is that banks may not pursue these activities when it leads to a dangerous conflict of interest, creates instability in the individual bank or the entire United States' financial system, or opens up the banking institution to dangerous trading strategies or involvement with risky assets.

Banks of certain sizes must report and disclose all of their covered trading activities to the appropriate government regulators. The bigger banks had to create programs that guaranteed they were abiding by the new rules. Besides this, their new compliance programs were subject to further independent analysis and tests. Institutions which were smaller were subjected to fewer reporting and compliance rules and regulations.

Western Union

Western Union proves to be a world-leading provider of global payment options and services. They help customers who range from individuals and families, to small businesses and not for profit NGOs, to international corporations. The company does more than simply help businesses and individuals to move money; they help national and international economies to expand and communities to experience a more prosperous and better life.

For the full reporting year 2015, Western Union transferred more than $150 billion dollars between customers and businesses around the globe. The firm boasts an impressive 500,000 different agents' locations, with more than 100,000 of their own ATM's and kiosks found around over 200 different countries and territories of the globe. They are constantly seeking to find smarter and better, more innovative and cutting edged means of sending money utilizing mobile, digital, and retail channels by providing a vast range of options for convenient pickup or payout to help their consumers and businesses with their cash needs.

Western Union is a major player in the world of currency translation as well. Their transactions happen throughout over 130 different currencies between more than a billion individual bank accounts around the world. They average an impressive 31 different transactions for every second (per the year 2015).

By simply going down to a retail outlet or utilizing the Western Union website or mobile app, customers are able to move money from almost any location to almost any other domestic or international location, from one currency to almost any other, and all in a matter of minutes. This helps their customers to be able to send money out to their family members or friends in almost every corner of the globe. They can offer financial support and encouragement, empower an education or entrepreneurial opportunity, or simply honor someone for a special accomplishment or occasion.

Their flagship service for individuals who wish to send money across the globe is called WU Connect. This international cross border system allows for peer to peer sending of funds to over 200 different nations and territories around the world. Pickup can be arranged via a wide variety of approved bank accounts, Western Union physical agent locations, and select mobile wallets.

Business customers also have access to a toolbox full of helpful services. The main category for this is the Western Union Business Solutions platform. This enables businesses to navigate their way through the challenging global economy. They can avail themselves of risk management, international payments, and cash management tools. More than 100,000 medium to smaller business clients, financial institutions, NGOs, and educational institutions are able to effectively transact in and make payment across national borders and through widespread geographical time zones.

Larger businesses and multinational corporations which require help in hedging international currency movements for the future are able to take advantage of their Leverage Forward Contracts. These help them to lock in an attractive current day exchange rate for specific time frames that extend up to 12 months out from the present date. This assists multinational corporations and big businesses in safeguarding their profit margins against currency movements over the short to medium term time frames. The WU system allows clients to place market orders in any time of the day or night. They can even set up a monitoring order to wait for a targeted advantageous exchange rate, whether or not they are sitting at their desk in the physical office or not.

The businesses can also avail themselves to the services Western Union offers to manage a company's exposure to foreign currency. Risk can be first identified and then addressed using a four step risk management protocol. The company maintains a staff of well-trained and knowledgeable specialists who are able to help set goals and develop a simple yet effective currency hedging plan to reduce and control currency exposures while protecting the important margins of profit.

Wholesale Banking

The concept of wholesale banking pertains to those banking services which are done between merchant banks or commercial banks and various other financial institutions. This form of banking services has to do with bigger bank clients like enormous corporations or other financial institutions. In contrast, retail banking concentrates on individual clients and small businesses. Such particular banking services cover financing of working capital needs, currency conversions, large trade transactions, and a range of alternative and specialized banking services.

There are so many different avenues which wholesale banking covers. This specialized department within the mega banks handles capital markets products, integrated credit, and a range of different advice and guiding for risk management, funding needs, and investment products and services for international and domestic major corporate clients. Such products and services run the gamut of structured transactions, specialized finance, credit structuring, loan syndications, project finance and securitization, merchant banking, wholesale equities, and public sector financing of infrastructure projects.

Among the many different types of wholesale banking clients are corporations which are medium sized to large, institutional investors and clients, pension funds, governmental departments and agencies, and other global banks and financial institutions both domestic and abroad. The services which they often need in day to day operations include equipment financing, cash flow management, large loans, trust services, and international merchant banking.

The concept also relates to lending and borrowing between larger institutional banks and other financial organizations. Such lending mostly goes on in the interbank market and revolves around huge sums of money in practice.

The majority of commercial banks function as such merchant bank operations, providing wholesale banking services besides the more usual retail customer banking services. It makes it more convenient for those customers who require wholesale banking services, as they will not be required to track down and go visit a specialized financial institution. Rather they are able to deal with the same bank which handles the customer's individual retail banking needs.

The most understandable means of comprehending this wholesale banking phenomenon is to draw parallels with a discount superstore chain such as Sam's Club or Costco. These outfits trade in such enormous quantities that they are able to feature special deals and lower fees per dollar of sales. For bigger institutions or organizations, this makes it advantageous for them who possess high dollars of assets and business banking transactions to participate in this banking wholesale instead of going the more traditional retail banking customer services route.

As an example, many businesses possess numerous locations throughout the country. They often times require a solution for their cash management, which wholesale banking can easily provide. Technology companies are an especially relevant business line for this type of banking. Perhaps an SaaS firm owns 10 sales offices throughout the U.S. It might be that every one of its 50 sales department members needs their own access to the company's corporate credit card. The company owners also insist on every one of the regional sales operations maintaining at least $1 million in cash reserves on hand. This amounts to $10 million worth throughout the various offices combined. Companies with these type of needs will be too big for the traditional format of ordinary retail banking.

The owners of this company might instead contact a significant sized bank and ask for a corporate account which will handle each of the company's financial accounts. These services function as a facility which will provide discounts to the company in exchange for meeting a minimum dollar level cash reserve requirements as well as a minimum level of monthly bank transaction requirements. It is in fact easy for the SaaS company to hit such targets each and every month. This is why the company will seek out such a corporate facility in order to properly consolidate together each of its financial bank accounts so that it may effectively reduce its total fees. This makes so much more sense for a larger company than instead having 10 different regional bank checking account and 50 separate retail bank corporate credit card accounts.

Zero Balance Account (ZBA)

The zero balance account, also known by its acronym ZBA, refers to the type of checking account which maintains a permanent balance of zero. The account does this through an automatic transfer of funds out of a master account. The amount which transfers over only proves to be sufficient enough to cover any and all checks which other financial institutions present to the bank where the holder's account resides.

Corporations utilize these zero balance accounts in order to draw down excessive balances from separate accounts. It also helps them to keep better and stricter control over amounts they disburse in the ordinary everyday course of business operations.

These accounts will therefore only have a zero balance within them. The only exception to this zero balance account status is when checks are written against them and presented to the bank in question. In this way, companies are able to keep the balances as close to zero for accounts that do not have any reason to hold excessive reserves. The activity in these ZBA's is restricted to only processing payments. This is why they do not maintain any ongoing balances.

Because of this, a larger sum of funds will remain available for the company to deploy. They can instead put them to work in investments and company cash flow purposes rather than keeping low dollar amounts lying idly by in a number of sub-accounts. It does not present a problem when checks must be paid off from these special zero balance accounts, since the electronic clearing system recognizes that these accounts are in fact ZBA's and they will move the necessary funds over from the master account at the financial institution in the precise dollar amount needed to clear the check.

Companies and other organizations can also rely on a zero balance account to fund purchases which employees make with their debit cards. This allows them to carefully monitor all of the financial transactions and any activities which take place on the cards, since the debits must be pre-authorized. This works well for companies and charitable not for profit organizations which are protected by not maintaining any idle funds within the ZBA's.

The debit card transaction will not be approved by the bank which backs them until and unless the requisite funds become available to the account by a transfer from the authorized account representative at the firm or NGO. This means that debit card transactions simply can not be run without prior authorization by the appropriate superior in the organization. Businesses are able to reduce their risks of activities which are not approved of occurring.

This is critically important to especially larger organizations with many employees and numerous sub accounts and associated corporate debit cards. There is no better spending control oversight for these types of situations than the zero balance account. Incidental charges can be monitored throughout the sizeable operations.

Since incidental expenditures are variable in nature, it is harder to fund and control them without such an account. Large companies and not for profits effectively reduce rapid access to the company or charitable funds with these debit cards. In this way, they have put into place the best practices for approval procedures. It ensures that such procedures will be adhered to in advance of a purchase being made by an employee.

As budget monitoring tools, these ZBA's are also ideal. They may be established as one account per department or business operation. This allows the accountants at the company an easy and fast means of monitoring annual, monthly, and even weekly to daily purchases. The company book keepers are also able to effectively track particular shorter term projects and their financial expenditures by utilizing such a ZBA. Projects which are in jeopardy of running significantly and rapidly over budget also benefit from such accounts. The overseers can maintain control of all purchases by requiring proper approval and notification before the charges take place.

The master account of such zero balance accounts is the critical component of this entire concept. As the central operational center for all fund management in the organization, the account will be employed to disperse funds to all ZBA subaccounts as needed. These master accounts typically include other benefits like better interest rates for balances which they hold.

HARP Program

HARP stands for the Home Affordable Refinance Program. This program that the government sponsored entities Fannie Mae and Freddie Mac created and back is unique. It turns out to be the one refinancing program that works with borrowers who are eligible and who have no or little equity in their houses so that they can receive refinancing benefits and lower interest rates.

The HARP program has changed some over the years. One of the main improvements to the program was to get rid of the underwater limitation amount for home owners. There is now no restriction on how much more the borrowers owe on their mortgage than the property is actually worth.

Thanks to this modification in the HARP program, a great number of home owners who could not qualify before will now be able to do so. The program itself expires on September 30, 2017. This makes it important for buyers who are considering it to take action on it or get more information in the near future.

The HARP program is a good choice for those borrower who have maintained a successful payment history over the last 12 months. It does not require a perfect payment record. Over the last six months there can not be any late payments. From six to twelve months prior there can only be a single payment that is 30 days late. The loan must also be guaranteed by or owned by Freddie Mac or Fannie Mae.

In order to participate, there are several other considerations. The loan only can be modified with this HARP program if it is either the primary residence or a second house or investment property. It makes most sense if the value on the house has declined. It is especially useful for those whose first mortgage amount is greater than the present house market value or if there is little equity in the property. The loan will only qualify if borrowers closed on them before or on May 31, 2009. This information can be obtained with the loan lookup tool and results on the Fannie Mae or Freddie Mac websites.

There are a number of good reasons for borrowers who are not able to take advantage of other refinancing means to utilize the HARP program on their mortgage. It lowers the monthly payment after the process is complete. The refinance procedure also decreases the interest rate. This means that borrowers will save on interest as well as monthly payment amounts.

It can be especially beneficial for those who have adjustable rate mortgages. These HARP interest rates are fixed, which means they will not change with time. Lower interest rates and less interest also help the home owners to build up their equity faster. It is possible to get a refinanced mortgage with a shorter term as well. Because the program does not require any appraisals, this saves the home owners both money and time that it takes to find someone to perform them to most banks' satisfaction.

Participating in the HARP program is not difficult. It requires that borrowers undergo an application process, receive approval, and finalize closing much like with the original mortgage. HARP lenders work with the home owners every step of the way and assist in deciding if the program meets the needs of the borrower. There may be closing costs associated with the refinance. These often can be rolled over into the new loan to reduce out of pocket costs as necessary.

Home Equity Loan

A home equity loan is a means for home owners to borrow money using the value of their house. Borrowers find these loans appealing because they can usually borrow significant sums of money. Besides this, they are much simpler to get approved for than with many competing kinds of loans. A home owner's house secures these home equity loans. The borrowers may utilize these funds for any purpose that they wish. They do not have to be spent on expenses related to the house that secures the loan.

Such a home equity loan is actually a kind of second mortgage on a house. The first mortgage allows the buyer to purchase the home. When sufficient equity is established in the house, owners can attach other loans to the property to borrow against it.

There are a number of benefits to obtaining a home equity loan. They appeal to both lenders and borrowers. Borrowers get better APRs or interest rates from them than with other loan types. Because they are secured by the value of the home, they can be easier to get approved for even with bad credit. The IRS allows home owners to deduct interest expenses from these home equity loans from their taxes. Finally, borrowers are able to obtain substantial loan amounts using these loan vehicles.

The lenders like these loans because they consider them to be safer loans. The house acts as collateral in the process. This means that banks are able to seize the house to liquidate it and regain unpaid balances if the owner fails to make the payments. Because of this, banks know that borrowers will make the payments of these loans a high priority so they do not lose their house.

Banks protect themselves in any case by not lending too much against the value of the property. In general, lenders will not allow borrowers to obtain a greater amount than 85% of the value of the house. This includes both the amount that remains on the first mortgage as well as the second mortgage home equity loan. This percentage is known as the loan to value ratio. It can vary somewhat from one bank to the next.

The way home equity loans work is relatively straightforward. Borrowers receive a one time cash payment. They then make fixed payments each month to pay back the loan over a pre-set amount of time. The interest rate will be set by the bank at the beginning of the loan. With every payment, the loan balance declines after part of the interest costs are covered. This makes these amortizing loans.

Sometimes borrowers do not require all of the money at one time. An alternative to the home equity loan in this case is the HELOC home equity line of credit. This delivers a set amount of money which home owners can draw on only when and if they require it. The borrowers only have to pay interest on money which they physically draw and borrow. It is possible for the interest rate to change on these HELOC loans. Banks may also cancel such a line of credit before the borrower has utilized all or part of the funds.

Home equity loans can be used for many different needs. It is wise to improve the value of the house with the money through renovating, remodeling, or increasing the appeal of the property. Other common uses borrowers employ them for are to help pay for a second home, to afford college tuition and expenses for family members, or to consolidate bills with high interest rates.

ING Group

The ING Group is the largest Dutch and Benelux based bank in the world. The acronym ING translates into International Netherlands Group in English. This global bank and financial institution draws on its important European base to provide services on a global scale. Their customers include governments, institutions, major corporations, smaller businesses, families, and individuals. ING is famous for its world class service and well known brand that put their customers at the center of all their endeavors.

Over 52,000 staff work for the ING Group to deliver wholesale and retail banking and financial services and products to their customers located in more than 40 countries. The group calls its advantages the important financial positions it enjoys, its international network, and its all channel distribution strategy. They claim their greatest asset is their brand that is both well recognized and well liked by customers in a number of different countries. They are honored as one of the leading institutions found in the Banks industry sector of the Dow Jones Sustainability Index.

The ING Group acts as a European network bank that extends its range around the globe for its many customers. They boast a range of global franchises as well. ING concentrates on growing into the main bank for new customers. This strategy is to increase the number of customers with recurring income payment accounts that have another product minimally included. ING starts customers with retail banking and offers other anchor products such as lending, wholesale banking transactions, and investments.

The bank's business transformation program is working to help the bank grow into an optimal operating model of Wholesale Banking. To do this, they are increasing their customer base in industry transaction and lending financial services. To better focus on this goal, they divide their principal and target markets into market leaders, challengers, and growth markets.

The market leaders group are those countries of Benelux - the Netherlands, Belgium, and Luxembourg. These are the nations where the ING Group is market leading in wholesale banking and retail banking services. The strategy here is to expand in certain segments and to continue developing into their direct first bank model. They are investing in digital capabilities and providing excellence in their operational programs to this effect.

Challenger markets are those where they are working consistently to increase their current market share. These markets include the important countries of Germany, France, Italy, Spain, Austria, and Australia. The businesses in these nations provide wholesale and retail banking. The focus with retail here is to offer online direct banking services. This gives them a price advantage versus other traditional banks.

In the challenger markets, ING is working to use their already recognized savings vehicles to grow into payment accounts and to create primary banking relationships. They are striving to launch from their expertise in direct banking to build up the consumer lending and small to medium sized business lending. They are also working on diligently increasing their corporate customer base in these countries through new abilities in industry lending and transaction services here.

ING Group's growth markets include their businesses in Turkey, Poland, Romania, and Asia. Here they provide a comprehensive line of wholesale and retail banking. These rapidly expanding economies provide them with solid opportunities for growth. This is why they are investing heavily to build a sustainable market share here. To do this, they are concentrating their efforts on digital technology leadership and also are pushing their direct first bank model.

Japanese Bankers Association (JBA)

The Japanese Bankers Association is also known by its internationally recognized acronym the JBA. This is the elite financial institutions' umbrella organization. Its membership is comprised of bank holding companies, banks, and banker associations throughout Japan. Their purpose is to promote planning for the best operating of payment systems, to reinforce compliance and promote CSR, to encourage appropriate transactions for consumers, and to support the individual banking endeavors and operations of its member banks.

Every year the Japanese Bankers Association elects both a chairman and a number of vice chairmen to oversee the organization. It is the JBA's Board of Directors which confers each March to hold this election. The various board members actually vote to decide who will become the two heads of the umbrella banking organization. President and Chief Executive Officer Takeshi Kunibe of Sumitomo Mitsui Banking Corporation is the current chairman of the JBA, as of February 2017.

In Japan, the various financial institutions are actually broken down into a few important categories. These groupings come from characteristics which include either the historical backgrounds or the primary business functions of the institutions in question. Such categories include city banks, regional banks, and member banks from the Second Association of Regional Banks (or regional banks level II). These are not legally binding definitions. Instead they are classifications used to help with publishing statistics and administration efforts.

City banks prove to be extremely large in their geographical representation and size. Their headquarters lie in the major cities of the Japanese islands. They also boast branches in the important and large population centers of Tokyo, Osaka, and other important cities and surrounding suburbs. Today there are only five of the large and impressive city banks remaining in Japan. These are as follows: Bank of Tokyo-Mitsubishi UFJ, Resona Bank, Mizuho Bank, Sumitomo Mitsui Banking Corporation, and Saitama Resona Bank. Mergers and acquisitions in the field have helped to narrow this important category down from the original 13 city banks to the present five.

By contrast, regional banks are typically found and headquartered within the primary city of a given prefecture in Japan. They naturally conduct the overwhelming majority of their business endeavors in their home regional prefecture. It follows that they would have important local ties with area governments and locally based businesses. Today's Japan boasts 64 regional banks such as Hiroshima Bank, Shikoku Bank, and Bank of Okinawa.

The final category of the Japanese based banks is the regional banks level II. Such financial institutions tend to provide services to individuals and smaller companies in their principal geographical regions. The vast majority of the Regional Banks II was once mutual savings banks at some point. There are 41 Regional Banks II in Japan today. Among them are banks including Towa Bank, Aichi Bank, and Ehime Bank.

The banking classification picture has become more clouded in 1999 with the rise of certain specialty financial institutions which were not traditional banks at all. These entered into the banking universe in Japan through founding different kinds of banks like those which are internet based or specialize in settlements. They do not fall under a traditional category of the three mentioned above and so are referred to by the Japanese Bankers Association as "other banks." There are five banks in this non-traditional banking category. These are as follows: Citibank Japan, Aozora Bank, Norinchukin Bank, Shinsei Bank, and Seven Bank.

There is only one single foreign based banking member of the Japanese Bankers Association today. This is the United States' headquartered JP Morgan Chase Bank, National Association. Citibank Japan is of course classified as one of the "other banks" so does not fall under this category as determined by the JBA.

One of the primary ancillary functions of the Japanese Bankers Association is to calculate up and publish the JBA TIBOR. Since 1995, they have released this Japanese Yen TIBOR rate as well as the Euroyen TIBOR rate from 1998. Such rates reveal the unsecured call markets' prevailing rates as well as the interest rates on the offshore market.

Mortgage Backed Securities (MBS)

Mortgage backed securities turn out to be a special kind of asset which have underlying collections of mortgages or individual mortgages that back them. To be qualified as an MBS, the security also has to be qualified as rated in one of two top tier ratings. Credit ratings agencies determine these ratings levels.

These securities generally pay out set payments from time to time which are much like coupon payments. Another requirement of MBS is that the mortgages underlying them have to come from an authorized and regulated bank or financial institution.

Sometimes mortgage backed securities are called by other names. These include mortgage pass through or mortgage related securities. Interested investors buy or sell them via brokers. The investments have fairly steep minimums. These are generally $10,000. There is some variation in minimum amounts depending on which entity issues them.

Issuers are either a GSE Government Sponsored Enterprise, an agency company of the federal government, or an independent financial company. Some people believe that government sponsored enterprise MBS come with less risk. The truth is that default and credit risks are always prevalent. The government has no obligation to bail out the GSEs when they are in danger of default.

Investors who put their money into these mortgage backed securities lend their money to a business or home buyer. Using an MBS, regional banks which are smaller may confidently lend money to their clients without being concerned whether the customers can cover the loan itself. Thanks to the mortgage backed securities, banks are only serving as middlemen between investment markets and actual home buyers.

These MBS securities are a way for shareholders to obtain principal and interest payments out of mortgage pools. The payments themselves can be distinguished as different securities classes. This all depends on how risky the various underlying mortgages are rated within the MBS.

The two most frequent kinds of mortgage backed securities turn out to be collateralized mortgage obligations (CMOs) and pass throughs. Collateralized mortgage obligations are comprised of many different pools of securities. These are referred to as tranches, or pieces. Tranches receive credit ratings. It is these credit ratings which decide what rates the investors will receive. The securities within a senior secured tranche will generally feature lesser interest rates than others which comprise the non secured tranche. This is because there is little actual risk involved with senior secured tranches.

Pass throughs on the other hand are set up like a trust. These trust structures collect and then pass on the mortgage payments to the investors. The maturities with these kinds of pass throughs commonly are 30, 15, or five years. Both fixed rate mortgages and adjustable rate ones can be pooled together to make a pass through MBS.

The pass throughs average life spans may end up being less than the maturity which they state. This all depends on the amount of principal payments which the underlying mortgage holders in the pool make. If they pay larger payments than required on their monthly mortgages, then these pass through mortgages could mature faster.

Prime Rate

The Prime Rate is the most typically utilized shorter term interest rate for the United State banking system. All kinds of lending institutions in the United States employ this U.S. benchmark interest rate as a basis or index rate to price their medium term to short term loans and products. This includes credit unions, thrifts, savings and loans, and commercial banks.

This makes the Prime Rate consistent around the country as banks strive to be competitive and profitable in their lending rates which they provide to both consumers and businesses. A universal rate like this simplifies the task for businesses and consumers as they shop around comparable loan products that competing banks offer. Every state in the country does not maintain its own benchmark rate. This makes a California Prime or New York Prime identical to the U.S. Prime.

Commercial and other banks charge this benchmark rate to their best customers. These are those clients who have the best credit ratings and loan history with the bank. Most of the time banks' best clients are made up of large companies.

The prime interest rate is also known as the prime lending rate. Banks typically base it on the Federal Reserve's federal funds rate. This is actually the rate that banks loan money to each other for overnight purposes. Retail customers also need to be aware of the prime lending rate. It directly impacts the lending rates that they can access for personal and small business loans as well as for home mortgages.

The federal government and Federal Reserve Bank do not set the prime lending rates. The individual banks set it. They then utilize this base rate or reference rate to set the prices for a great number of loans such as credit card loans and small business loans.

The Federal Reserve Board releases a statistics called "Selected Interest Rates." This is their survey of the prime interest rate as the majority of the twenty-five biggest banks set it. It is this publication which reveals the Prime Rate periodically. This is why the Federal Reserve does not directly set this important benchmark rate. The banks more or less base it on the target level of the federal funds rate that the Federal Open Market Committee sets and changes at their monthly meetings.

Different banks adjust their prime lending rate at the same time. The point where they change it is generally when the Federal Open Market Committee adjusts their own important Fed Funds Rate. Many publications refer to this periodically changing reference rate as the Wall Street Prime Rate.

A great number of consumer loans as well as commercial loans and credit card rates find their basis in the prime lending rate. Among these are car loans, home equity loans, personal and home lines of credit, and various kinds of personal loans.

The rates above the prime lending rate that banks charge their less then prime (or subprime) customers depend on the credit worthiness of the borrower in question. The banks attempt to correctly ascertain the risk of default for the borrower. For the best credit customers who have lower chances of defaulting, banks can afford to assess them a lower interest rate than others. Customers with higher chances of defaulting on their loans pay larger interest rates because of the risk associated with their loans not being repaid.

As of June 15, 2016, the Federal Open Market Committee voted to maintain its target fed funds rate in a range of from .25% to .5%. As a result of this, the U.S. prime lending rate stayed at 3.5%. Once per month the Federal Reserve committee meets to determine if they will change the fed funds rate.

Reserve Requirement

The reserve requirement proves to be the quantity of funds which banks are required to hold on hand each and every night. This is expressed as a percentage of the bank's total demand deposits. A country's central bank is responsible for setting out the effective percentage rate.

Within the United States, it is up to the Federal Reserve's Board of Governors to determine the member banks' reserve requirements. Such a requirement is applicable for commercial banks, savings and loan associations, savings banks, credit unions, Edge corporations, U.S. based branches or agencies of foreign banks, and agreement corporations.

The banks are allowed to keep their cash physically within their proprietary on-site vaults or keep them deposited with their area Federal Reserve Bank. When banks lack sufficient cash to fulfill their reserve requirements, they are able to borrow cash from other banks with extra to spare. They could also obtain a loan from the discount window of the Federal Reserve alternatively. Money which banks lend or borrow from one another in order to meet their own requirements is called the Federal funds.

Among the many tools which the Fed counts at its disposal, the reserve requirement is the underlying basis for all of them. They are able to employ this to precisely control cash liquidity within the economy. Smaller reserve requirements prove to be expansionary types of monetary policy. This is because they permit a greater amount of money to flow through the banking system into the real economy. Higher reserve requirements conversely are contractionary. They soak up money from the pool of available liquidity and tamp down on economic activities.

It is also true that the greater a reserve requirement is, the smaller the profits will be for a bank deploying its customers' money. Higher requirements are particularly challenging for smaller banks. This is because they begin with a smaller pool from which to lend out money. Because of this reality on the ground, small banks are usually exempted from such onerous requirements. Smaller banks are those which have fewer deposits than $12.4 million.

The Fed does not often actually change the reserve requirement. This is because it is expensive to do so. Banks are forced to rectify their policies to compensate when this is done. Because of this, the board avoids changing the requirements on its member banks. It is far easier for them to tweak the amounts of deposits which are subjected to the various reserve requirements every year.

For example, since October 12, 2012, the Federal Reserve has mandated that every bank possessing greater than $79.5 million in deposits must keep a minimum reserve amount of 10 percent of total deposits. Those banks which count under $79.5 million but still greater than $12.4 million only have to keep three percent of deposits on hand. Again those banks with fewer than $12.4 million in deposits fall under the pre-determined exemption amount. They enjoy a zero percent reserve requirement.

The Federal Reserve does raise the levels of deposits which are subject to its various ratios each year. This provides the banks with an incentive to become larger. From June 30 to June 30, the Fed is able to raise its low reserve tranche and accompanying exemption amount by 80 percent of the amount that deposits increase in the previous year.

Deposits which are considered for these reserve requirements include a number of different types. These are automatic transfer service accounts, demand deposits, NOW accounts, telephone or authorized transfer accounts, share draft accounts, ineligible bankers' acceptance, and affiliate-issued obligations which mature in seven or fewer days. Banks are only required to accept the net amount. They are not expected to cover any amounts owed to them by other banks or any cash that remains outstanding. As of December 27, 1990, deposits do not comprise Euro-currency liabilities or non personal time deposits.

Securitization

Securitization is a financial engineering procedure. In this process, sponsors take an asset or group of assets that is illiquid and turn them into a saleable security. Mortgage backed securities are common instruments that result from securitization. These MBS products are backed by assets. The security that underlies them are a group of mortgages.

The securitization process works in a series of steps. It begins with a bank or other financial institution originating a number of mortgages. The mortgages themselves are backed up by the specific properties the home buyers purchase. Next, these single mortgages become combined together into what is known as a mortgage pool. The pool of mortgages remains in trust for the MBS collateral.

MBS are sometimes put together in the securitization process by an investment bank or other third party independent financial firm. They could also be issued by the original bank that underwrote the mortgages in the beginning. Large aggregators like the government sponsored entities Freddie Mac, Fannie Mae, and Ginnie Mae put together many of these mortgage backed securities themselves.

Whichever group undertakes the effort, the end result is identical. Securitization creates a new financial security that is underpinned by the legal and financial claims on the assets of the mortgagors. Sponsors then take the new security and sell it investors or other interested parties in the secondary mortgage market. This proves to be a very large and liquid market. It offers substantial tradability to the securitized mortgages that would have little to no liquidity as stand alone investments.

When these mortgage backed securities are being created through the securitization procedure, issuers have options. Many times they decide to break up their pool of mortgages into a group of different components. They call these tranches. With tranches the issuers are able to put together the security however they would like.

This means they can craft one MBS into a range of tolerance for risk. Some buyers like pension funds are only interested in investing in mortgage backed securities with high credit ratings. Other investors like hedge funds have a higher tolerance for risk. They will be willing to take on tranches with lower credit ratings in exchange for higher returns.

Individual investors who want to participate in these mortgages have several choices. They can take a participation certificate share in a pool of mortgages. This pass through participation provides a pro rated share of interest and principal payments that come back into the pool when the issuers obtain the borrowers' monthly payments. There are also pools of such pass through mortgages called CMOs collateralized mortgage obligations.

Many individuals would like to become involved in mortgage investing but are unsure of all the research involved with the various kinds of MBS. An ideal way to participate without having to understand the detailed mechanics is through mortgage mutual funds. These funds could invest in a single kind of MBS like a Ginnie Mae issued one.

Still other funds are comprised of a range of mortgage backed securities as part of a group of holdings in government bonds. Mutual funds provide a better diversification in loan holdings than individuals might afford on their own. They also offer the ability to reinvest all payments of principal and interest into other MBS. This helps to reduce the risks of changing interest rates and prepayments. It also permits investors to receive yields that vary with current interest rates.

Sub-prime Borrower

A sub-prime borrower is an individual who has credit that is considered to be less than perfect. This is the opposite of a prime borrower. Bankers call prime borrowers those who possess higher and better credit scores, low debt ratios, and significant incomes which are more than enough to cover their monthly bills and expenses.

Sub-prime borrowers often are only able to obtain sub-prime loans. These types of loans received the blame for causing the 2008 mortgage crisis. Despite this fact, the loans continue to exist today. They are an important part of post crisis lending, though so far they have not caused another financial crisis or global meltdown.

Those called sub-prime borrowers have many characteristics in common. These imply that the individuals are more likely to default on their mortgage loans than other individuals. Poor credit is the first element they share. This could be because they did not receive any opportunities to create a sufficient credit history.

It might also be from problems they had with making payments in the past. The dilemma for these borrowers is that they do not have many choices other than sub-prime lenders. This often traps them in a cycle of debt from which is difficult to escape. An under 640 credit score is considered to be sub-prime, though some lenders set the defining limit lower to even 580.

The sub-prime borrowers also have problems with their monthly payments. These payments are so large that they consume a significant part of the monthly income for the borrowers. This is determined in how high the debt to income ratio proves to be. A higher DTI ratio means that the borrowers do not have enough money to cover bills if they suffer a drop in income or have unanticipated expenses arise. Loans can still be approved in some scenarios when the borrowers' present debt load is significant.

The cost for a sub-prime loan is another thing these borrowers share together. These forms of mortgage loans usually cost more since lenders do not want to assume additional risk without higher compensation. Predatory lenders have used this limited ability to receive loan approvals in order to prey on borrowers with no other choices. These higher expenses manifest in a few different ways. It might be junk application and processing fees, greater interest rates, and penalties for early prepayment which prime borrowers seldom pay.

Risk is the dominant theme for sub-prime borrowers, lenders, and loans. Because the loans have a lower chance of being paid back, the lenders exact more in fees and higher rates. These greater costs cause the loans to be riskier for the borrowers as well. Debt is difficult to retire when higher interest rates and costs come with it.

Sub-prime borrowers should try to avoid these expensive and debt trapping loans whenever they can. Staying out of such costly credit is essential for individuals to not drown in debt. This is easier said than done when people are put into the sub-prime category. There are not as many options to comparison shop for the loans. There are also fewer options for alternative kinds of loans to use for the needed financing.

If these borrowers are able to make themselves look less risky to the various lenders, it will improve their chances of escaping from these types of loans. This may mean some credit repair work needs to be done before individuals with credit challenges make applications for loans.

Sub-prime Lender

A sub-prime lender makes loans to customers who fall into the sub-prime borrower category. These products often include loans which are normally considered to be standard. They are structured for and marketed to borrowers who possess inadequate income, lower credit scores, and a higher debt to income ratio. These borrowers can not qualify with lenders regarded as traditional.

Sub-prime lenders are often willing to issue loans to customers with special circumstances. These include those who possess less documentation of income, high LTV loan to value ratios, and sometimes a combination of the two. This type of lending is considered to be aggressive and overly risky for most traditional financial institutions.

Where mortgages are concerned, sub-prime lenders are still providing basically the same product in the form of a 5/1 ARM adjustable rate mortgage or a 30 year fixed rate mortgage. The main difference is that the rate which accompanies such a product will be considerably higher.

There are other types of mortgage loans that some observers include in this category as well. Among these are negative amortization loans, interest only loans, and non fixed interest rate mortgages. A great number of analysts consider FHA loans to be in the subprime category. This is because their highest allowable LTV is 96.5% while they accept a credit score minimum of 500.

Sub-prime lenders will also make loans for other assets and in other categories besides housing and mortgages. In fact they issue them for practically all financing needs. This includes credit cards, car loans, unsecured personal loans, and student loans.

After the financial crisis that started with sub-prime mortgages, the government enacted a number of laws protecting consumers from these predatory types of finance. It has made it more difficult to find sub-prime house loans since then. There are a great many of the original loans from before the crisis still in existence. Besides this, sub-prime lenders have found means of circumventing them and giving approval to loans that fall into this category.

Borrowers can take many actions to avoid being a victim of a sub-prime lender. Managing credit carefully is among the most important. It is free to check all credit reports for accuracy. Borrowers can fix errors. Consumers should also deal with any defaults or missed payments if they can. Rebuilding credit requires some time, but going through the process will help borrowers to be considered more prime to lenders.

There are many newer lenders these days that are considered to be legitimate. Online searches and online lenders have opened a whole new avenue to consumers trying to avoid sub-prime loans. Some of these online lenders appeal to those with poor credit and still provide acceptable rates.

There are also peer to peer lending services. They can be more flexible with borrowers than the traditional credit unions and banks often are. It is always a good idea to research any lenders which consumers consider before providing them with important personal information or paying any fees.

Borrowers who are struggling to avoid these sub-prime lenders can also look into a co-signer on a loan. It can help credit challenged borrowers to receive approval from a lender which is traditional and offers better rates. These co-signers put their own credit at stake and take a big risk in doing so.

Sub-prime Mortgage Crisis

The sub-prime mortgage crisis proves to be a still going financial and real estate crisis. It continues to revolve around the steep decline that you saw in American housing prices, the resulting increase in numbers of mortgage delinquencies and finally foreclosures, and the ultimate fall of securities that are backed up by these sub-prime mortgages.

The problems began with the fact that around eighty percent of all United States mortgages that banks gave out to sub-prime borrowers, or people with less than perfect credit, turned out to be adjustable rate types of mortgages. Housing prices actually reached their highest point in the middle of 2006 and then began sharply falling. This caused refinancing of interest rates on mortgages to be harder to obtain. The double edged sword of adjustable rate mortgages resetting at their higher rates started, causing an enormous number of delinquencies and finally foreclosures in mortgages.

The greater problem came as these mortgages underlay a number of financial securities that many financial firms held in huge numbers. They saw most of their value disappear in the following months. Investors around the world then began to dramatically cut back on the quantities of collateralized debt obligations and other mortgage securities that they bought. Besides the damage that increasing sub-prime mortgage delinquencies and foreclosures created themselves and for the investments based on them, this sub-prime mortgage crisis led to a fall in the ability of the banking system to engage in lending. This caused significantly tighter credit and lower rates of growth throughout the developed world, in particular in Europe and the United States,that are still plaguing the industrial countries.

Ultimately, the sub-prime mortgage crisis arose as a result of easy up front loan terms which banks made to borrowers. Both the borrowers and the banks felt confident that the loans could be easily refinanced into better terms as needed, since housing prices were steadily rising over a long term trend. Financial incentives were provided to sub-prime mortgage originators.

This coupled, with fraud that borrowers and lenders engaged in, significantly boosted the quantities of sub-prime mortgages to customers who should have received standard conforming loans or who should not have received loans at all. When the easy interest rate terms expired, the majority of sub-prime loan holding consumers could not refinance at the better rates in which they had believed. The interest rates reset higher, dramatically increasing the monthly mortgage payments.

Home prices started falling to the point that homes were no longer even worth as much as the original mortgage, meaning that they could not be sold to pay off the mortgage obligation. Instead, the borrowers' best interest lay in going through foreclosure and walking away from the hopelessly underwater homes. This continuous epidemic of foreclosures that began with the sub-prime mortgage crisis is still a major continuous part of the world wide financial and economic crisis. The foreclosures are still taking away wealth from consumers and sapping away at the damaged banks' balance sheets.

Trust Account

A trust account refers to a type of account which a trustee holds on the behalf of the beneficiary. The trustee does not have the ability to utilize the funds in any personal capacity, but merely to safe keep, disburse, and invest them for the advantage of the beneficiary.

An example of this type of arrangement is when an attorney holds funds for the benefit of the client. The attorney will not be able to draw upon the funds until after a certain protocol takes place. As the attorney earns the lawyer fees, the client will have to first review and then actually approve the bill from the attorney before he or she can transfer the client funds from this trust account over to the general account of the attorney for settlement of bills.

There are a number of reasons and situations in which individuals may opt to establish a trust account. In some scenarios, people wish to disperse a pre-determined sum of money to their family or other loved ones over a number of years or throughout the remainder of their natural lives.

As a real world example, consider the following. Parents may wish to establish some trust accounts which will provide money to their dependents and/or children every month if and when they die. In such a scenario, it would normally be banking brokers who would manage such accounts. In fact these broker trustees would draw down the account values by the appropriate amount every month or year as they disbursed the either monthly or yearly funds to the beneficiaries for the individuals who originally formed the trust.

There are other common kinds of trusts as well. One of these is a property tax trust account. Such accounts will be established by entrepreneurs of real estate who own a variety of properties. Rather than have to be concerned about the property tax funds and disbursements to the appropriate taxing authorities themselves, they elect to form a trust account which will pay the taxes. This prevents the entrepreneurs from forfeiting their valuable properties because they forgot to pay the property taxes. There are a number of monetary benefits to having such an account. One of these is that estate taxes will not apply to properties contained in such a trust when the owner dies.

There are two different main types of trust accounts. These are revocable and irrevocable trusts. With revocable trusts, these represent deposit accounts whose owners chose to name one or several beneficiaries. These beneficiaries would then obtain the deposits in the account once the holder of the account died. As the name implies, such revocable trusts may be terminated, revoked, or altered on demand whenever the holder of said account wishes. In this particular case, the owner is the trustor, settlor, or grantor of the revocable trust in question. These types of trusts will be established as either informal or formal. While trustees are powerful and have a broad scope of authority over the assets of the beneficiary, they are not omnipotent, but must be bound by the laws and regulations of the jurisdiction which pertain to trust accounts.

Irrevocable trusts on the other hand are similarly deposit accounts but they are not titled in the name of the owner. Instead these become titled as an irrevocable trust for the name. The owner, trustor, settlor, or grantor also makes deposits of money or other valuable assets to the trust account. The principal difference is that the owners forfeit all ability to alter or cancel the trust once they have established it. These types of trusts also become created once an owner of a revocable type of trust dies. They can be set up through a judicial order as well, or even by a statute as appropriate.

Trust Fund

A trust fund proves to be a specific kind of legal entity. It contains property or cash which it holds to benefit another group, individual, or organization. Numerous different kinds of trusts exist. They are governed by almost as many provisions that determine how they work. Every trust fund involves three critical parties. These are the grantor, the beneficiary, and the trustee.

A grantor is the individual responsible for creating the trust fund. Grantors can do this with a variety of assets. They might give stocks, bonds, cash, mutual funds, real estate, private businesses, art, or other items of value to the fund. They also determine the terms by which the trustee will manage the fund.

Beneficiaries are the individuals who receive the benefit of the fund. The grantor sets it up on their behalf. The assets the grantor places inside of the trust fund are not the property of the beneficiary. The trustee oversees them so that the financial gain benefits this individual according to the rules laid out by the grantor at the time he or she establishes it.

Trustees are the managers of these funds. They could be an institution like a the trust department of a bank, an individual, or a number of trusted advisors. Their job is to make sure that the fund fulfills its duties spelled out by the governing law in the trust documents. Trustees typically receive small management fees. The trustee could manage the assets directly if the trust specifies this. In other cases, trustees have to pick out investment advisors who are qualified to manage money.

Trust funds come to life under the rules of the state legislature where the trust originates. Different states offer advantages to certain types of trusts. This depends on what the grantor wants to do by establishing the fund. This is why attorneys help to draft the trust documents to make sure they are correct and most advantageous. As an example, there are states which allow perpetual trusts that can continue forever. Other states make these illegal because they do now want to enfranchise a class of future generations who receive substantial wealth for which they did not work.

Special clauses may be inserted into these trusts. Among the most heavily used is the spendthrift provision. This keeps the beneficiary from accessing the fund assets to pay debts. It also allows parents to ensure that any irresponsible children they have do not find themselves destitute or homeless despite poor decisions they may make.

Trust funds provide a large number of benefits. They receive special protection from creditors. They ensure that family members follow wills after the grantor passes away. These trusts also help estates to avoid as many estate taxes as possible so that wealth can reach a greater number of generations.

Trusts can be an ideal way to ensure the continuity of a business. Sometimes business owners wish to protect a company and their employees after they die. They might still wish for the profits to benefit their heirs. In this case, the trustee would oversee the management of the business while the heirs reaped the financial rewards but could not break up or ruin the company through mismanagement.

Trusts can also be used with life insurance to transfer significant amounts of money which will benefit the heirs. A small trust could purchase a grantor life insurance. When the grantor dies, the insurance money funds the trust. The trustee will then buy investments and give the rents, interest, and dividends to the beneficiaries.

Variable Interest Rate

Variable Interest Rate refers to the applicable interest rate which comes with a security or loan. When such rates are variable, it means that they will fluctuate up or down in time. The reason for this is that a specific index or interest rate benchmark underlies them. This rate or index will change from time to time in the natural course of events. There is a potential great benefit to having such a variable interest rate when this index or interest rate goes down. This is because the interest payments of the borrowers will similarly decline. On the other hand though, when such underlying benchmarks go up, the interest payments will also rise, sometimes painfully.

Not every loan, mortgage, or security will utilize the same benchmark index or interest rate as its underlying comparison point with these Variable Interest Rates. In fact it actually comes down to the kind of security or loan in question. With credit cards, car loans, or mortgages, the Variable Interest Rates are often based on the prime rate for the nation in which the loan is based. Naturally the financial institutions, lenders, and banks will assess a spread between their rate and the true benchmark rate. The amount of this spread form of fee depends on many factors. Some of these are the credit rating of the individual getting the loan and the kind of asset to which the loan is attached.

Where credit cards are concerned, most of them work on a Variable Interest Rate arrangement. Their APR annual percentage rate happens to be fixed to a specific interest index. In most cases, this is the prime rate. With the prime rate, it generally moves up or down in lockstep alongside the federal funds rate that the United States Federal Reserve sets as part of their fiscal and monetary policy tools. A move up or down in this rate eventually leads to a net change in the underlying interest rate of credit cards across America. Such rates for these credit cards working off of variable interest rates are able to shift up or down at will. The credit card companies are not even required to provide written or verbal advance notice to their cardholding customers before adjusting the rates when the benchmark moves.

In the accompanying terms and conditions of such credit card accounts, the applicable interest rates will generally be described as the underlying prime rate added to a certain percentage rate. This specified additional percentage is always heavily based upon how credit worthy the card holding individual proves to be. As a real world example, many cards will assess an interest rate addition of 10.9 percent on top of the prime rate to come up with their credit card customer interest rates.

With other forms of loans that have Variable Interest Rates, the payment schedule proves to be different. The majority of non-credit card forms of loans are actually installment loans. These payments to repay them are fixed and pre-arranged. This leads to the loan reaching pay off on a pre-set specified day. All that changes as interest rates rise or fall is the amount of the payment. This will similarly increase or decrease per the amount of the interest rate change as well as the numbers of payments that remain to fully pay off the loan.

Mortgages have their own specific features. When they carry Variable Interest Rates, such loans are known as ARM adjustable rate mortgages. A great number of such ARMs actually begin their repayment life with a fixed lower interest rate during the initial years of the loan life. Once this pre-determined time frame expires, they will adjust up, sometimes steeply. The most typical periods of fixed interest rates on these adjustable rate mortgages turn out to be either three or five years. Loan officers refer to this as 5/1 or 3/1 ARMs.

Wire Transfer

A wire transfer is the quickest, safest, most reliable means of sending money within the United States, in other countries, or around the world. They are often essential in the more critical financial activities of life such as purchasing a house. The reason larger transactions occur in this form of payment is because the recipient can receive and verify the funds transfer the same day it is done, or as near to immediately as possible (besides Western Union and Money Gram, which cost substantially more to utilize).

A wire transfer actually represents a means to electronically transfer money from one party to another via a bank as intermediary. A traditional and typical wire transfer starts at a credit union or bank and electronically processes through either Fedwire or SWIFT networks. Another common name for such a wire transfer is a bank wire, which also encompasses the standard bank to bank transfers.

Ultimately the wire transfers have become so successful and utilized throughout the United States and rest of world simply because they are capable of moving even enormous sums of money to any destination bank in the world in only a day or two. If they are affected within the same country such as the United States then same day wires can be done. For an international transfer via wire transfer, it often requires another day or even two to complete.

Since the funds move rapidly through the financial system, recipients are not required to wait a material amount of time for the funds to become cleared. This means they can access and utilize the money without significant delays. No holds are typically placed on wire transfer monies. The safety issue means that merchants prefer the wire mechanism. This is because checks can bounce because of insufficient funds, while wires never do so. In other words, these are guaranteed funds.

There are some particular requirements that wire transfers need in order to be possible to transact. At least in the United States, both parties would require a functioning bank account in order for a bank to act as intermediary. Since thieves can not open a bank account too easily, nor bank anonymously in the United States, it is difficult for them to carry out scams using bank wires. This is because it leaves a paper trail which is easy for law enforcement officials to follow.

This does not mean that wire transfer scams are unknown entirely. It is possible for a person to be tricked into wiring money to a fraudster for a purchase or service they never receive. Examples of this are fake insurance policies or false retirement or investment products. Once the wire has cleared the recipients account, they can either withdraw the funds in person or wire it to an offshore overseas account.

By the time the victims realize that they have been scammed, the funds sent by wire will be long gone. They would no longer be recoverable by traditional U.S. law enforcement or even court order methods once they have been transferred offshore. Pulling money back after it has been dispatched via bank wire is extremely difficult in any case. This is true even if the funds remain in the recipient's bank account.

Wire transfer fees can be significant. In many parts of the United States, they run as high as $40 to dispatch a bank wire. Many banks charge upwards of $10 in order for a bank wire to be received into an account. The costs to send one are higher if the wire is funded by utilizing a credit card cash advance. Cash advance fees would then apply, as well as typically large interest rates, plus the wire transfer fee. This is why it is typically most financially sound to effect a bank wire directly from the sender's bank account.

World Bank

The World Bank proves to be an institution in international finance. It offers developing countries of the planet leveraged loans to help out with funding capital programs. The major goal is to cut down on poverty. Every decision that the organization enacts is required to be carried out with the objectives of encouraging international trade, foreign investment, and facilitate capital investment.

The World Bank should not be confused with the World Bank Group. The World Bank is two of the five organizations within the World Bank Group. These two groups that make up the World Bank are the IDA, or the International Development Association, and the IBRD, or International Bank for Reconstruction and Development. The World Bank Group is also made up of MIGA, or the Multilateral Investment Guarantee Agency; the IFC, or International Finance Corporation; and the ICSID, or International Center for Settlement of Investment Disputes.

The World Bank's two organizations are widely supported by the nations of the world. The International Development Association contains one hundred and sixty-eight members, while the International Bank for Reconstruction and Development is comprised of one hundred and eighty-seven countries. Exclusively members of the IBRD may belong to the various other organizations in the World Bank. All IBRD members are supposed to belong to the IMF, or International Monetary Fund, as well.

The year 2010 saw significant revisions to the allocated votes of members of the World Bank. Developing countries, especially China, gained a larger voice. The nations that possess the biggest voting power currently are the United States at 15.85%, Japan at 6.84%, China at 4.42%, Germany at 4%, Great Britain at 3.75%, and France at 3.75%.

These changes are called the Phase Two of the Voice Reform. They also gave major votes percentages to countries such as India, Brazil, Mexico, and South Korea. To come up with the extra votes, the voting percentages of the majority of developed nations declined. Russia, the United States, and Saudi Arabia's votes did not change.

The World Bank focuses on reducing the poverty found in the poorest developing countries in the world. They do this analyzing a nation's economic and financial condition and comparing it against a snap shot of many local groups in the country. Then it comes up with unique strategies for addressing the problems of the given country. After this, the country's government lays out their biggest priorities for reducing poverty, so that the World Bank can line up its help to work together with this government.

Besides giving out money to the poorest countries on the earth, the World Banks heads several other initiatives. They are managers of the Clean Technology Fund. They also run the Clean Air Initiative.

www.ingramcontent.com/pod-product-compliance
Lightning Source LLC
Chambersburg PA
CBHW051210170526
45166CB00005B/1837